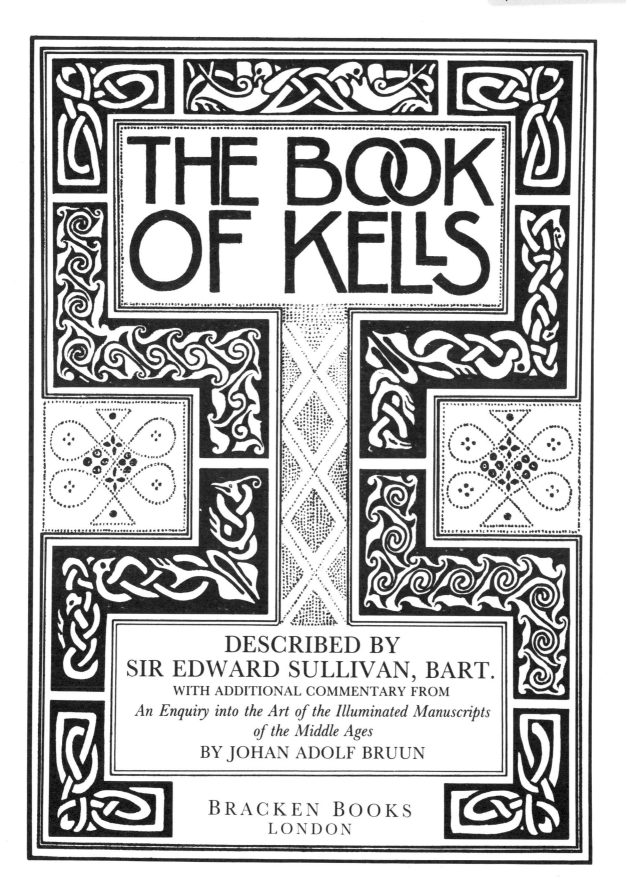

THE BOOK OF KELLS

DESCRIBED BY
SIR EDWARD SULLIVAN, BART.
WITH ADDITIONAL COMMENTARY FROM
An Enquiry into the Art of the Illuminated Manuscripts
of the Middle Ages
BY JOHAN ADOLF BRUUN

BRACKEN BOOKS
LONDON

This is a facsimile reprint of
The Book of Kells, second edition,
originally published by The Studio
Ltd, 1920 with additional material
taken from *An Enquiry Into The Art
of the Illuminated Manuscript of the
Middle Ages*, by Johan Adolf Bruun.

This edition was published in 1986
by Studio Editions, a division of
Bestseller Publications Ltd,
Princess House, 50 Eastcastle St,
London W1N 7AP, England

ISBN 1 85170 035 8 (cased)
ISBN 1 85170 196 6 (paperback)

Copyright © Studio Editions, 1986
Reprinted Bracken Books, 1988

Printed and bound in Hong Kong

PREFATORY NOTE

THE Editor desires to acknowledge his indebtedness to the late Rev. Dr. Abbott, Librarian of Trinity College, Dublin, who kindly gave permission and every facility for the reproduction of the pages from the Book of Kells which appear in this volume. Special thanks are due to the Sub-Librarian, Mr. Alfred de Burgh, whose invaluable assistance and untiring pains in revising the reproductions at various stages of the work reduced very considerably the difficulties with which the engravers were faced. As mentioned by Sir Edward Sullivan towards the end of his Introduction, the compound letters shown in the last five plates are from remarkably clever copies made by the late Mrs. John R. D'Olier. Her son, the late Mr. Isaac D'Olier, kindly placed the copies at the disposal of the Editor for reproduction in the present volume.

To those who have not examined the Book of Kells two features in the plates may require explanation ; viz., the cut margins, which in some cases have damaged the designs ; and the variation in the tones of the backgrounds. Both these defects are present in the original manuscript. The first, as explained on page 6 of the Introduction, is due to the ignorance of some incompetent binder to whom the priceless volume was entrusted about one hundred years ago ; and the second is caused by discolouration, for which age and the fact that the Manuscript was for some time buried under the soil are probably responsible.

PREFACE TO THIRD EDITION

Since the first and second editions of this consideration of *The Book of Kells* were written, some important publications have made their appearance the contents of which would seem to call for something more than a passing notice. Chief, and most recently published, amongst them, is Dr J. Bröndsted's *Early English Ornaments*, London and Copenhagen, 1924. Mr Reginald A. Smith, of the British Museum, in his Preface to the translated edition, expresses, in generous terms, his opinion of the value of the work in view of the close relationship between all branches of the Teutonic world during the period treated of. The work purports to be an attempt, not hitherto made, 'to give a comprehensive account of the origin and development of art in England in the 400 years which lie between the introduction of Christianity and the Conquest, with this limitation, however, that two domains of the art practice of the period, the figure art and interlaced designs, are left out.'

Anyone can readily understand the reason for these particular omissions who has had an opportunity of making himself acquainted with the monumental work of Professor Baldwin Brown, *The Arts in Early England*, London, 1903–1921, a series of volumes which completely cover all that need be said or illustrated in the domain of interlaced art. I shall refer later on to some extremely interesting observations arising from a new comparison between the art of the Book of Kells and that of its great rival, the Book of Lindisfarne, which forms part of the concluding volume of the series.

Dr Brönsted's work, in so far as it relates to the vine-pattern design, its origin, development and general adoption in the British Isles, whether in monumental carvings or in illuminated manuscripts, is undoubtedly the result of extended research and close observation. If anything, it is possibly overdone so far as that particular form of embellishment became a feature of manuscript illumination—for, although it undoubtedly held a prominent position as a decorative distinction on the crosses of this country, it was by no means equally prominent in the illuminations of manuscripts. For instance, Brönsted is found to say (page 85): 'Finally, in Irish art regions, we find the vine of north England both with and without animals in the Book of Kells (see Fig. 71), a fact which is not without its bearing on the question of the date of the ornamentation of the north of England.' But when we come to examine his own illustration of the figure referred to we find that it does not represent the vine pattern at all, the foliage, so far as it can be called so, being the very conventionalized trefoil which is so frequently found interwoven with the Kells forms of decoration. Dr Brönsted seems, at times, too satisfied that the decorative features of monumental crosses moved *pari passu* with the embellishments of the illuminations: 'It can only be due to the chances of survival that the north English ornament is in our days to be found practically exclusively upon the crosses. The rest of the art and art industry in the north of England at the time must naturally have had a corresponding aspect and have worked with similar decorative material'. This is, to my mind, a belittlement of the extraordinary artistic range of which the Irish school of illuminators were pre-eminently possessed; and it must have been because of some such similar fancy that Dr Brönsted, in another place, has had to assume—when he cannot prove—that the sculptured figures on the well-known Bewcastle and Ruthwell crosses are the outcome of imported foreign colonists: 'That these advanced and admirably executed sculptures, dated from shortly after A.D. 700, should be the work of native Anglo-Saxon stone-carvers, I consider absolutely out of the question, and what has been alleged in support of this view, most recently by Baldwin Brown, is, in my opinion, irrelevant.'[1]

Again, on page 35: 'A colony of Oriental artists, called in by ecclesiastics, may, in the course of the latter part of the seventh century, have established themselves in the north of England; the colony founded a school, and its mode of ornamentation was adopted by Anglo-Saxons and practised by them through a century and a half with constant modifications and conventionalization.'

As regards the vexed question of the approximate date of the Book of Kells, several arguments were advanced by me—some of them entirely new—in my earlier prefaces. I can find but few suggestions in Dr Brönsted's work which throw anything that can be called light on this very interesting topic, one in every way worthy of his admittedly rare powers of research and investigation. Having stated that the Kells Manuscript is, by the latest researches, generally placed early in the eighth century (page 71), he is content to add, in a note, the names of some of those who hold that view (with references to their works) and goes on: 'Sullivan, *The Book of Kells* (Studio 1914) pages 29–39[2] keeps still to the old untenable position that the manuscript is necessarily dated IX–X by its leaf ornamentation.' The mighty Homer must, indeed, have been having 'a goodly nap' when he penned so misleading and unfounded a state-

1 Professor Baldwin Brown's argument *contra*, with which I am in complete accord, will be found, in *The Arts in Early England op. cit.*, volume V, pages 287—89 and 306—13.

2 This edition, page 41 *et seq.*

ment. The 'leaf ornamentation' is a very trivial point in connexion with my argument, which runs (as mentioned in the note) to many pages. Again, when he attributes to me a suggestion that I ever mentioned the *tenth century* as a possible date for the Kells Manuscript, he is merely dreaming of something which he had not read. The argument I brought forward (and for the first time) based upon the square or rectangular punctuation which distinguished the Kells volume from any other more or less contemporary manuscript of which I am aware, was one to which one might reasonably look for some scholarly reply from any careful student of early Irish palæography. Other grounds on which I based my views were connected with (a) the unfinished portions of the manuscript, (b) the contraction marks employed in the Latin text, and (c) the robe ornamentation of triangular groups of dots so frequently made use of. The dismissal of all these by the mere word 'untenable' can hardly be looked on as anything but uncritical—so much so, indeed, as to leave a reader somewhat doubtful as to the value of a good many of the author's other theories. To take the matter of the square-shaped punctuation prints alone, I have made considerable searches amongst the works of well-known palæographers, and up to the present have to confess with some surprise that I cannot find even one of them who has a word to say on that special shape, which is one of the prominent distinguishing features of the system of punctuation made use of in the Book of Kells. I had examined some original manuscripts and many of the reproductions which were available before writing my introduction to that Manuscript, and my conclusion then was that the square punctuation form was practically unknown in Latin script before the beginning of the tenth century, with the solitary exception of the Book of Kells. Recent further researches have only confirmed my opinion as to the late introduction of the square type of pointing, and also with regard to its value and importance in connexion with the date of the Manuscript itself. I have found no cases where the square type is employed before the eighth century. In the tenth century one begins to see traces of its use, for instance, the Cædmon manuscript,[1] A.D. 1000, which I had an opportunity of examining at the Bodleian Library last year, does contain some examples of square punctuation; while the *Encyclopædia Britannica*,[2] 1911, gives some lines of 'particularly fine writers of the twelfth century' from *Leviticus*, A.D. 1176, where, if the reproduction is to be relied on, there are in one line alone three distinct examples of the square-shaped pointing. In all the circumstances I am forced to the conclusion that the Book of Kells must be considered a *post* eighth century produc-

1 Now reproduced in facsimile, with introduction, by Sir Israel Gollancz, 1927.
2 Volume XX, page 577.

tion until some manuscript of an earlier date is found in which the punctuation marks are distinguished by the square form so obvious in the Kells volume.

By universal acknowledgment, the two finest examples of Irish or Hiberno-Saxon illumination are the Book of Kells and its only rival, the Book of Lindisfarne. A comparison between the details of these two volumes is, naturally, full of interest to a student of the Kells Manuscript, more particularly when we remember that no one knows with any certainty which of them was the earliest to see the light. Professor Baldwin Brown has written some highly instructive pages on this comparison to which readers may be referred with every confidence.[1] A serious preliminary question between the two MSS is based on the strong divergence of opinion that exists amongst the chief authorities as to whether or not the Book of Lindisfarne is the outcome of the Northumbrian school of illumination or the work of a purely Irish artist. The matter is too deep and complicated for discussion here, and one can only say that of the latest writers on the subject Professor Baldwin Brown is altogether in favour of pronouncing the Lindisfarne an Anglo-Saxon work, while Dr Bröndsted[2] is equally emphatic in declaring it to be 'a purely Irish work in its ornamentation.' Professor Brown undoubtedly goes into the question at much greater length than his opponent. His opponent, too, praises the manner in which the differences in style between the two famous Irish MSS are set out, but adds: 'I see nothing in that difference which entitles us to call the Book of Lindisfarne Northumbrian . . . The whole animal and line ornamentation in the Book of Lindisfarne is as truly and characteristically Irish as anything can be; the difference between its illumination and that in the Book of Kells rests singly and solely on the difference between two individual ways of aesthetic feeling.'

One of Professor Baldwin Brown's arguments in favour of a Northumbrian provenance is thus expressed: 'In one detail also we distinguish an Anglian trait, and this is in the delight in the bird form which is far more in evidence in the Durham book than in the Kells or other Hibernian manuscripts. The creature, we have seen, is a cormorant, and cormorants breed on the Farn Islands . . . There is nothing improbable in the idea that the birds so loved of the Northumbrian designer are the sea fowl of his own Lindisfarne. . . .'[3]

In tracing the actual origins of both animal and floreated forms of ornament, an immensity of industry has been devoted to the subject generally, as well as to the multifarious forms into which such embellishments have shaped themselves both in monumental and illuminative art, in different countries and

---

1 *The Arts in Early England, op. cit.*, volume V, chapters XV and XVI.
2 *Early English Ornaments, op. cit.*, page 92.
3 *The Arts in Early England, op. cit.*, volume V, page 376.

changing periods of time. Interesting as such researches may be to those who are absorbed in their pursuit, the results tend largely to a bewildering confusion where even the searcher not infrequently finds himself in a maze of contradiction from which a satisfactory exit becomes well-nigh impossible. Professor Baldwin Brown has some excellent and common-sense observations on the point with which I am in complete agreement. 'All through history', he says,[1] 'the designer of good ornament has worked on a basis of convention and has depended far less on copying from nature and on symbolism than literary critics imagine. . . . This is not the way the ornamentalist works. The forms he uses are as a rule derived from tradition, though they may be modified and enriched by the action of his individual taste and fancy as well as at times by details borrowed freshly from nature. The general scheme in the foliage panels on the crosses is the long established one of the undulating scroll, originating it seems in the Mycenaean period, in which the main stem gives out offshoots alternately to right and left that intersect the spaces with their curves and terminate in leaves, flowers, or branches of berries or fruit . . . not copied directly from nature nor selected for any reason of symbolism. The main scheme, on the other hand, is reminiscent of a symbolical motive. It is based on the vine, a floral motive that comes into vogue in the Hellenistic period and that was taken over with avidity by the early Christians with whom it carried a symbolical significance as the True Vine, the birds and animals feeding upon the grapes having a far-off reference to the faithful nourished on divine food.'

The following observations from the pen of a well-known palæographer are well worth bearing in mind when endeavouring to trace the origin of any particular form of design incorporated by Celtic artists in either illumination, sculpture or bronze:

'The great difficulty in understanding the evolution of Celtic art lies in the fact that although the Celts never seem to have invented any new ideas, they professed an extraordinary aptitude for picking up ideas from the different people with whom war or commerce brought them into contact. And once the Celt had borrowed an idea from his neighbour, he was able to give it such a strong Celtic tinge that it soon became something so different from what it was originally as to be almost unrecognizable.'[2]

I have drawn attention in an earlier preface to a very remarkable use made of the triangular groups of red dots which are so frequently employed in the Book of Kells for the embellishment of the robes of holy persons. I find now that there are some few examples of a similar practice to be found in the

1 *Op. cit.*, volume V, page 273.
2 J. Romilly Allen, *Celtic Art in Pagan and Christian Times*, London, 1904.

x

Gospels of Mac Durnan (at Lambeth) and that Westwood[1] gives its date as 'not later than the beginning of the eighth century' although Dr Todd had dated the manuscript as of the century before. The portrait of St John in his Mac Durnan manuscript shows clearly the triangular groups of red dots both on the robes of the Saint as well as being used for general purposes of decoration.

Another Irish manuscript should be mentioned here, the Latin Psalter in St John's College, Cambridge, which Westwood dated eighth or ninth century. It contains a most weird illustration of the Crucifixion, 'unquestionably the most ancient specimen of Irish pictorial composition which has hitherto been given to the public. . . . The extraordinary propensity of the Irish School for marginal rows of red dots . . . will be evident from the drawing of the Saviour's habiliments, eyes, ears, etc.'

Strange to say the dots here are only marginal, and do not appear on the robes.

One cannot, therefore, without further evidence, rely very strongly on the dotted robes in the Book of Kells as indicating any special or traditional practice—a view to which I was formerly inclined—and as the only other instance I have observed of what I may call the Kells use of dots for the decoration of robes is of a later date and in no way connected with holy persons,[2] it must be the task of some other inquirer to discover what is the real meaning of the practice which is undoubtedly well established in the Kells manuscript.

Both Bröndsted and Baldwin Brown have a good deal to say concerning the arrival of scholars from foreign places into Ireland in very early Christian days. A good summary of the history of that important movement is to be found in quite a recent work, from which I take the following extract.[3]

'Many extravagant things have been written about the Irish Golden Age: but in the sober scholar's prose of Bede, the story is miraculous enough. That fierce and restless quality, which had made the pagan Irish the terror of western Europe, seems to have emptied itself into the love of learning and the love of God: and it is the peculiar distinction of Irish medieval scholarship and the salvation of literature in Europe that the one in no way conflicted with the other . . . '[4]

---

1 *Palæographia Sacra Pictoria.*

2 See Baldwin Brown *op. cit.* III, 374, plate LXXII (No. 1) representing an officer of the Court of Charles the Bald in which both sleeve and tunic are adorned with traingular group of dots (about A.D. 840).

3 Helen Waddell, *The Wandering Scholars*, 1927.

4 Poole, *Illustrations of Mediæval Thought*, page 10, *et seq.*

Zimmer[1] has a theory that Ireland, secure from invasion in the shelter of the Four Seas, had long been a refuge of the timid scholars of Gaul, driven like thistledown before the barbarian blast, and that even in the fifth century the Irish schools were notable. There is support for it in a casual reference by Columbanus to the judgment of Irish scholars in the fifth century on Victorinus of Aquitaine, the philosopher.[2] At any rate, by the sixth century the Irish schools were the most famous in Europe. The scholars came by the old trade routes, the three days' journey from the Loire to Cork[3]—in 550 a ship-load of fifty landed there—or up the Irish Sea to Bangor. That such a one 'forsaking his own country sojourned in Ireland for the love of God and of learning' becomes a commonplace of biography. Bede, writing of the great plague of 664, speaks of its ravages among the scholars: 'many of the nobles of the English nation and lesser men who also had set out thither, forsaking their native island either for the grace of sacred learning or a more austere life. And some of them indeed soon dedicated themselves faithfully to the monastic life, others rejoiced rather to give themselves to learning, going about from one master's cell to another. All these the Irish willingly received, and saw to it to supply them with food day by day without cost, and books for their studies, and teaching, free of charge.'[4]

EDWARD SULLIVAN, 1925

---

1 Zimmer, *Glossæ Hibernicæ*, 1881, and *The Irish Element in Mediæval Culture* (translated), 1891.

2 *Epist.*, i Migne, LXXX, c., 261.

3 Bröndsted, so far as my recollection goes, does not mention this approach to Ireland.

4 Bede, *Hist. Eccles*, iii, 27.

PREFACE TO SECOND EDITION

THE success which has attended the publication of this work is, for two reasons, a source of much satisfaction to those responsible for the original issue of the book. In the first place, it amply justifies the belief, entertained by the producers when the work was brought out, that the presentation of a series of the unrivalled illuminated pages of the Book of Kells, in their actual colours, would be regarded as a welcome supplement to such previously published works on the same subject as contained only uncoloured representations ; and secondly, it establishes the fact that there are many more persons—outside the world of connoisseurs, archæologists and palæographers—who are interested in the Manuscript itself, its history, and its artistic details, than was popularly believed to be the case. Since the date of the first issue, some six years of war and the turmoil that follows war apparently put an end to all serious investigations in the domain of Celtic palæography. No new light, so far as I am aware, has been thrown during those years on any disputed questions relating to the Book of Kells. Consequently there is little to add, from the studies of others, to the description of the Manuscript as given in the first edition. The Manuscript itself is, however, so full of information from within, that a slight study of even the reproductions given in this volume enables a careful observer to discover features of interest, previously unnoticed, on almost every page. Amongst such discoveries, made by myself, are a few perhaps worth mention.

I suggested in 1914 that the square-shaped punctuation marks, which are a characteristic of the Manuscript, might have some bearing on the vexed question of its date. What I have since noticed has considerably strengthened my original surmise. For instance, in Plate X. (lines 2 and 7) will be seen examples of the three-dot full stop which is frequently used to end a sentence throughout the work. It will be noticed, however, that in close and somewhat puzzling proximity to these stops there are other very similar dot-formed groups, actually on the line of the text, which, at first sight, might easily be taken for punctuation signs. They are in reality only ornaments ; and the dots are in every case *round* in form, whereas the true punctuation marks are always rectangular. The fact that these two very similar forms are used on the same page, in conditions calculated to mislead a reader accustomed to the round forms of an earlier date, would seem to show that the Manuscript must have been written at a time when the transition stage was already past, and the square punctuation had definitely superseded the rounded form.

Besides this, there is another piece of internal evidence, as yet unnoted, which shows that the new system was firmly established when the Manuscript was written. The scribe occasionally *illuminates* the stops, enlarging them into decorative forms to harmonise with the general embellishment of the page. Plate III. contains three striking examples of this curious innovation. In the 2nd, 4th, and 7th lines from the foot of the page will be seen quaint ornaments of rectangular outline, intruding, as it were, immediately after the words " seniores," " profetissa," and " ihm." They have probably been regarded, up till now, as mere instances of the stray decorative features which are scattered broadcast through the whole volume. Their position, however, in places where a full stop is actually required, and where there is no trace of any other punctuation marks to be seen, shows them to be nothing more or less than enlarged forms of the single dot which was one of the recognised methods of indicating the end of a sentence in early Celtic manuscripts (see *post* p. 35). Plate X., at end of line 4, furnishes another example ; and Plate XV. contains yet another, though of much smaller proportions, following the word " mihi." These strange instances of decorated punctuation would seem to me to have been introduced deliberately with a view to drawing special attention to the recently adopted rectangular punctuation signs ; and it is hardly conceivable that liberties such as these would have been taken by any scribe unless the new system of pointing had been generally adopted at the time when he had the work in hand. If this be the case, it must follow that the date of the Manuscript should be ascribed to a period which cannot possibly be earlier than the latter end of the ninth century.

I have added a little to the Introduction bearing on the contest that continued for nearly a thousand years between the Byzantine and the Celtic modes of embellishment in the field of artistic illumination, and have touched, though lightly, on the superb results that sprang from the final union of the two contending forces. Also a few trivial oversights have been corrected in the letterpress of the original edition.

EDWARD SULLIVAN.

xiv

THE BOOK OF KELLS

INTRODUCTION

ITS weird and commanding beauty ; its subdued and goldless colouring ; the baffling intricacy of its fearless designs ; the clean, unwavering sweep of rounded spiral ; the creeping undulations of serpentine forms, that writhe in artistic profusion throughout the mazes of its decorations ; the strong and legible minuscule of its text ; the quaintness of its striking portraiture ; the unwearied reverence and patient labour that brought it into being ; all of which combined go to ma e up the Book of Kells, have raised this ancient Irish volume to a position of abiding pre-eminence amongst the illuminated manuscripts of the world. Many attempts have been made to reproduce its unique illuminations ; and, so far as form and outline are concerned, the reproductions have been as far as possible successful. But all such efforts have up till now failed to give a living representation of its marvellous pages—for without its colour harmonies no reproduction can be regarded as adequate from the point of view of art. The last important attempt at reproduction in colour was made about forty years ago ; but the scientific knowledge of the time was unequal to the strain sought to be put upon it. In the years which have since elapsed the science of light, photography, and colour-reproduction has made rapid advances towards an accuracy which was unknown when the earlier attempts were published ; and it is only by the aid of such advancement that the production of the present volume has become possible.

A word by way of Preface.

In this respect the work now published differs from all its predecessors ; for, though still distant from absolute perfection, the reproductions here given will be found to be infinitely closer to the originals in the important matter of actual colour than any of the so-called facsimiles which up to the present have been included in any published work. For this reason the present volume should not be regarded as in any sense a rival of the uncoloured reproductions which have already appeared of the Book of Kells. Its office is rather to supplement in colour what has already been accomplished by ordinary photography and monochrome ; to add a new value to previous efforts with the assistance of the most recent methods and processes of polychromatic photography and colour-printing. Looked at from ths standpoint one may fairly claim for the work here produced that it fills with some measure of satisfaction a gap in the pictorial history of Celtic illumination, and affords as it were a nearer view of one of the most interesting and beautiful manuscripts which have yet come from the hands of man.

The ancient town of Kells. The town of Kells, in County Meath in Ireland, lies some twenty miles west of Drogheda and the Irish Channel. It was known in days as early as St. Patrick's in the Latinised form of Cenondæ, bearing at a somewhat later date the name of Cenannus and Kenlis. Kennansa was its old Irish appellation. Within its narrow precincts to-day there are still standing three very ancient and well-known Irish stone crosses with characteristic carvings on them ; an old church, the rebuilt remains of which date from the year 1578 ; a round tower—one of the many to be found still in Ireland ; and a building which has long been described as the House of St. Columb.

Of the famous Monastery of Cenannus, or Kells, no trace remains— either of wall or foundation—but persistent tradition, with a strength that not infrequently outlasts both stone and mortar, has ascribed the founding of this vanished monastic institution to St. Columba. Irish historians have fixed the date of its foundation as about the year 550 A.D.

St. Columba, or Colum Cille. Columba himself, otherwise known as Colum Cille (*i.e.*, Columb of the Church), was born in the north-west of Ireland about 521 A.D. He is represented, according to ancient chronicle, as having resigned his hereditary claim on the Kingship of the island with the object of devoting himself to a monastic life. About the year 553 he founded a monastery at Durrow, in central Ireland, which became, as the Venerable Bede has stated, his most important establishment in that country. He withdrew from his native land to Iona in A.D. 563, which island, afterwards known as Hy-Columkille, became, through the missionary exertions of himself and his successors in the abbatial see, the radiating centre of Christian civilisation in the north of Britain, and the chosen burial place of the Kings of Pictland and Scotland. For this reason it is that Shakespeare, as we are reminded by Sir John Gilbert in his introduction to the " National Manuscripts of Ireland," tells us of King Duncan's body being

2

> carried to Colmekill,
> The sacred store-house of his predecessors,
> And guardian of their bones.
>
> *Macbeth*, ii. 4.

An ancient Irish legend gives the reason why St. Columba left his native land, and shows us, incidentally, a vivid picture of the militant churchman of those early days. During a sojourn with St. Finnan, in Ulster, Columba borrowed his psalter, and copied it furtively in his church, with the aid of miraculous light in the night time. Finnan demanded the copy, but Columba refused to give it up, and the matter was submitted for judgment to Diarmaid, Monarch of Ireland, at Tara. Diarmaid, with the rough and ready justice of a new Solomon, decided that as to every cow belongs her calf, so to every book belongs its copy. A sanguinary battle was the result ; but the copy remained with him who made it. It was known in later times as *Cathach*, from the Irish *cath*, a battle ; and was preserved with much veneration by Columba's kindred. This psalter is now in the collection of the Royal Irish Academy, Dublin.

However, whether Columba or another was the actual founder of this early centre of Irish Christianity at Durrow, the place does not seem to have attained any great importance until the opening of the ninth century, when the marauders from Northern Europe—Danes, Frisians, Norwegians, Swedes, Livonians, and such like—poured down upon the Irish ecclesiastical colony in Iona, *Invasion of the Norsemen.*

> and the godless hosts
> Of heathen swarming o'er the northern sea

drove the community of that island-sanctuary to seek a place of asylum further west.

Some time between A.D. 802 and 815, when Cellach, the nineteenth successor of Columba, was Abbot of Iona, he fled for refuge to the monastery at Kells, and with his aid a new town of Colum Cille was erected there ; and this, from that time forward, became the chief station of the Columban community—the Abbot of Kells being invariably acknowledged as the legitimate successor of St. Columba. The names of both Columba and St. Patrick are still legible on one of the ancient stone crosses to be seen at Kells. Colum Cille is commemorated as one of the three patron saints of Ireland on June the 9th, the anniversary of his death in the year 597.

Whether or not the famous Book of Kells, or as it is often called the Book of Colum Cille, was written and illuminated in the ancient town of Kells is a question still unsolved. The last few leaves of the Manuscript, which in all probability would have furnished us with full information as to scribe, illuminator, and place of origin, have been missing for many years.

Kells in the 9th and 10th centuries. The history of Kells and its Abbey from late in the ninth century to the end of the tenth is a tale of continuous struggle against foreign and domestic aggression.* In 899 the Abbey was sacked and pillaged. In 918 the Danes plundered Kells, and laid the church level with the ground. Rebuilt, it was again spoiled and pillaged by the Danes in 946. Three years later, Godfrey, son of Sitric, plundered the Abbey. In 967 the town and Abbey were pillaged by the King of Leinster's son, supported by the Danes; but the allied forces were assailed and defeated by Domnald O'Neill, King of Ireland. Only a year later the Abbey and town were despoiled by a united force of Danes and Leinster people; while in 996 the Danes of Dublin made yet another pillaging raid on both the town and Abbey.* How the Gospels of St. Columba survived this century of violence and spoliation it is impossible to say: we only know that they were preserved in the church at Kells in the *The MS. stolen in 1006* year 1006, when, according to the earliest historical reference to the Manuscript itself, "the large Gospel of Colum Cille" in its cover of gold studded with precious stones, "the chief relic of the western world," was stolen by night from the greater church at Kells, and found, after a lapse of some months, concealed under sods, destitute of its gold-covered binding.† It is not unlikely that most of the leaves now missing from the Manuscript disappeared at the same time.

Cambrensis describes a similar MS. Many of the palæographers who have made a study of the Kells Manuscript, agree in thinking that Giraldus Cambrensis has described this identical volume in a passage in his *Topographia Hiberniæ.* Writing in the twelfth century he gives an account of a wonderful manuscript which was shown to him at Kildare. He records that he had seen nothing more marvellous than the book in question, which, according to information given to him at the time, had been written from the dictation of an angel in the days of the Virgin (St. Brigit). Giraldus undoubtedly has described an illuminated manuscript of great beauty, which, so far as its general contents go, might have been the Book of

* Archdall's *Monasticon Hibernicum.*   † "Annals of Ulster," sub anno 1006.

4

Kells. He lavishes the highest praise on its brillant colouring, on the endless variety of its figures, on the elaborate intricacies of its interlaced ornamentation—all of which, as he tells us, one would be ready to pronounce the work of angelic, and not human skill. Going into minuter detail, he continues : " On one page you see the face of God, drawn in godlike fashion—in another, the forms of the Evangelists with either six, four, or two wings."* When it is remembered that Giraldus spent many years, early and late in life, as a student at the University of Paris, where it is probable he had become acquainted with a more modern type of illuminated miniatures, it seems difficult to believe that he could have been alluding in the last quoted passage to the more or less crude figure representations of the Saviour contained in the Book of Kells. Besides, there are no " forms of the Evangelists " to be found in the Manuscript as it exists to-day that have either six or four wings ;† nor, indeed, is there any convincing reason suggested why the Book of Kells should have been found at Kildare. It is perfectly obvious, too, from intrinsic evidence that the Kells Manuscript was produced at a period when Celtic illuminative art had reached its very highest development ; and it is therefore plain that *it* was not produced in the lifetime of St. Brigit (A.D. 453-523), whatever the volume may have been which Giraldus has described. Besides, it is hardly credible that Cambrensis, if referring to the Book of Kells, should have omitted all mention of the remarkable loss and recovery of the Manuscript, the details of which had in his time been well-known for at least two hundred years.

One can only conclude that the book which the historian did see was one of the many beautiful illuminated manuscripts that have since disappeared, though not the Kells volume ; and that commentators have been somewhat too ready to adopt without much investigation a theory for which there seems to be but very little evidential support.

At the time of the dissolution of the monasteries the establishment *The Abbey* at Kells was surrendered to the Crown by its last Abbot, Richard Plunket. *surrendered to* The instrument under which this surrender was effected, dated *the Crown.* 18th November 1539, is entered on the Rolls of the Chancery of

* Hic maiestatis vultum videas divinitus impressum ; hinc misticas evangelistarum formas, nunc senas, nunc quaternas, nunc binas alas habentes.

† If the words " Evangelistarum formas " can be made to refer to the Evangelistic Symbols (and not to the representations of the Evangelists), it is true that some of them have what seem to be four wings. In no case do they appear with six.

Ireland, 31 Henry VIII. The famous Manuscript of the Gospels itself, which seems to have survived in an almost miraculous fashion the unending incursions and pillage of many centuries, found its way shortly after the surrender of the monastery into the hands of one Gerald Plunket of Dublin, a kinsman possibly of the last Abbot. During the time the volume was in his possession he inscribed some notes which are still legible on its pages, showing that portions were lacking at the end of the book even in his day. On an early leaf he writes : " This worke doth passe all men's conyng that now doth live in any place. I doubt not there . . . anything but that ye writer hath obtained God's grace. G.P." Another of his notes, dated 27th August, 1568, purports to give the number of the leaves then in the volume ; but under these words Bishop Ussher has written : " August 24, 1621. I reckoned the leaves of this booke and found them to be in number 344. He who reckoned before me counted six score to the hundred. Ja Ussher, Midensis elect."*

The MS. comes to Dublin University Ussher, who was commissioned by James I. to collect antiquities relating to the British Church, acquired, amongst other rare possessions, the Book of Kells. It was included in the portion of his collection which was transferred to Trinity College, Dublin, five years after his death, in the year 1661 ; since which time it has been the chief treasure of the University Library. Housed as it then was one might have expected that a volume of so notorious, not to say sacred, a character would have enjoyed inviolable sanctuary. Unhappily, what Norseman and Dane had failed to effect in early and wilder centuries was accomplished by an ignorant and mischievous bookbinder, some hundred years ago ; and under the barbarous hands of this craftsman many of the outer margins of its priceless illuminations have been " trimmed " out of existence, as may be seen by looking at the Plates in this volume.

The MS. described. The Manuscript in its present state consists of 339 leaves of thick, finely glazed vellum, measuring, in their now cropped condition, 13 by 9½ inches. The number of lines of text to a page of the Gospels is in general not more than 19 nor less than 17, the space occupied by the

* " National Manuscripts of Ireland," J. T. Gilbert's introduction. The words *Midensis elect* refer to Ussher's recent election to the Bishopric of Meath.

6

writing being 10 by 7 inches.   On a few of the pages the writing is in a peculiar semi-cursive hand, but as a rule it is of the fine, clear character shown in Plates III. and X.

The first leaf—too rubbed to furnish a reproduction of a satis- *The Evangeli-* factory kind—is surrounded by an ornamental border, and is divided *cal Symbols.* vertically into two divisions, one containing a number of Hebrew words with their Latin equivalents, and the other occupied by the Evangelical Symbols.   These symbols, which were adopted at an early period in the history of Christianity, are as follows : The Man, or Angel, stands for St. Matthew, figurative of his emphasising the human side of Christ ; the Lion for St. Mark, as he has set forth the power and royal dignity of Christ ; the Calf, or sacrificial victim, for St. Luke, as his Gospel illustrates the priesthood of the Saviour ; and the Eagle for St. John, the Evangelist who soars to heaven, as St. Augustine puts it, and gazes on the light of immutable truth with keen and undazzled eyes.   In the present instance these are all unhappily much worn by attrition, but enough is visible to show that books are held by each of the symbolical figures.

The next eight pages are filled with what are known as the Eusebian *The Eusebian* Canons.   They take their name from Eusebius, Bishop of Cæsarea, a *Canons.* well-known Church historian.   Before his time a Harmony of the Gospels had been constructed by Ammonius of Alexandria, about A.D. 220, in which St. Matthew's Gospel was taken as the standard, and parallel passages from the other Gospels were set out side by side with it. Eusebius improved on his predecessor's plan ; his object being to set forth the mutual relation of the four evangelical narratives, and not merely to furnish illustrations to certain passages from other sources, as in the marginal references in modern Bibles.   The method of interpreting the lettering in these Canons, dependent as it is on certain sectional divisions of the Gospels specially devised by the author, is too intricate to go into here.

As will be seen in Plate I., the Eusebian Canons are written in narrow columns, framed as it were by decorative pillars on which a considerable amount of characteristic ornament has been lavished.   The open spaces above the pillars contain the Evangelical Symbols, agreeing in number with the number of the Evangelists in the several Canons. The decorative surroundings of these eight pages are different in each page.   In two cases the ornamentation is of quite a simple nature, and

7

little in keeping with the general character of this portion of the Manuscript.

Early Irish charters in the MS. The next few pages of the Manuscript would seem to have been left blank when the book was originally written. They now contain several charters in the Irish language, embodying grants of lands from King Melaghlin of Meath to the Abbey of Kells, the Bishop of Meath and the Church of Kells, dated between A.D. 1024 and the twelfth century. Their insertion on these pages was obviously intended to provide for their greater security. They have been printed by the Irish Archæological Society in the *Miscellany*, Vol. I., in the original Irish, with a translation and notes by Mr. O'Donovan ; and are believed to be the only extant specimens of legal deeds in the Irish language dating from before the Norman invasion.

Portrait of Virgin and Child. Fol. 7 V., which follows, contains the full-page illustration of the Virgin and Child (Plate II.), on which Professor Westwood remarks* :—

"This singular composition is interesting from the proof it affords of the veneration of the Virgin Mary in the early Irish Church ; the large size in which she is represented, as well as the glory round her head (which singularly bears three small crosses), evidently indicating the high respect with which the Mother of Christ was regarded. The infant Saviour, it will be observed, is destitute of the nimbus ; the chair or throne on which the Virgin is seated is not devoid of elegance, terminating above in the dog's head with an immensely elongated interlaced tongue.† The drawing of the whole is entirely puerile, whilst the ingenuity displayed in the intricate patterns of the sides and upper part of the drawing is quite remarkable. This singular interlacing of the limbs of human figures is peculiarly characteristic of the Irish MSS., and it is accordingly found in the Gospels of MacRegol and the Book of St. Chad. The instrument held by the Angel at the right hand of the foot of the drawing is worthy of remark, being analogous to one of the sceptres held by St. Luke in the Book of St. Chad."

* *Palæographia Sacra Pictoria.* Book of Kells.

† It is difficult to think that Westwood (and the late Dr. Abbott, who took the same view) can here be right. The dog in the Bible had a notoriously evil reputation, being "unclean" under the Old Law, and would hardly have been selected as an ornament for the Virgin's throne. The head can surely be no other than that of the Lion, which also appears at the end of two of the columns in Plate I., and is found as a border terminal in Plates VI. and XI., not to mention other places throughout the Manuscript. There may possibly be in Plate II. an allusion to Solomon's throne (1 Kings x. 19), where two lions had a place beside the stays of the seat.

The significance intended to be conveyed by the large size of the Virgin's figure finds a curious parallel in the sculptures still to be seen on the ancient monolith cross which stands close to St. Columba's house at Kells. The rude figure of Christ there represented is much larger than the attendant figures. It was a form of denoting importance frequently employed in early Irish art. A singular feature of this picture of the Virgin is the group of six persons whose heads are shown in the small panel crossing the framework at the right-hand side. They are all turned away from the principal figure. Westwood, who finds it difficult to comprehend the object of their introduction, says that he knows no other instance of such an addition in the miniatures of the Virgin and Child. It will be noticed that by some curious error both the feet of the Virgin are right feet, while those of the Child are both left.

The pages which follow, extending to folio 25, contain the " breves causæ " (*i.e.*, chapter headings), and " argumenta " (*i.e.*, summaries) appertaining to each of the four Gospels. Some of these pages are inscribed in a more recent hand and in variously coloured inks. This preliminary matter was a very frequent addition to Gospel MSS. of and about the period of the Book of Kells. Coming as it did immediately before the Gospel itself, it was not unnaturally made the subject of much fine illumination. The first of these introductory pages breaks out amidst a magnificent wealth of intricate illumination in the words " Nativitas XPI in Bethlem Judeae Magi munera offerunt et infantes interficiuntur Regressio " (" The birth of Christ in Bethlehem of Judæa ; the wise men present gifts ; the slaying of the children ; the return "). The more modern writing at the foot of the page, repeating these same words, is believed to be in the hand of Gerald Plunket, possibly a relative of the last abbot of the monastery of Kells. It was from him that the volume passed into the possession of Archbishop Ussher, from whom, as already mentioned, it came to the library of Trinity College, Dublin.

Fol. 19 V., depicted in Plate III., contains a portion of the " Argument " to the Gospel of St. John. This page, which contains some characteristic peculiarities common to early Irish manuscripts, reads as follows :—

Breves causæ and Argumenta.

> *exponitur ut sciendi desiderio collocato ET*
> *quaerentibus fructus laboris et deo magiste*
> *rii doctrina servetur*

9

ZACHA
riae sacerdotii appa
ruit angelus et adnuntiavit ei filium iohan
nem ET idem mariae adnuntiavit angelus
filium ihesum ℂ toribus ET acci
Nativitatem ihesu adnuntiat angelus pas
pit simeon puerum ihesum ET benedixit
deum et de anna profetissa ℂ bat
Annorum duodecim ihesus in templo doce
Seniores ℂ tismum poeniten
Ubi iohannis baptizat populum bap

The turn under the path. The symbol ℂ, known in Irish MSS. as " head under the wing " or " turn under the path"—which, as will be seen, occurs three times on this page—indicates that the words immediately following it are to be read after the end of the next full line. The first of the above passages in which it occurs will therefore read:—

adnuntiavit angelus filium ihesum Nativitatem ihesu adnuntiat angelus pastoribus ET accipit simeon, etc.

The " turn under the path " occasionally takes other shapes. A curious instance of its altered form is to be found in the "Pater Noster," fol. 297 V., where it appears at the beginning of the half line in the figure of a small man apparently in the act of jumping, with one of his legs cocked up and the other turned down towards the following line of the text.

From fol. 20 R. to 26 V. the text is much varied by the use of black, scarlet and mauve inks. In fol. 23, front and back, the writing is all in mauve, excepting the last line of the verso and the ornamental initials, while touches of red and yellow are introduced for decoration. This portion, in fact, presents us with a handwriting totally different from that which precedes and follows it. It looks as if the original had possibly been lost and was replaced by the work of a later and much inferior artist. The initials in these twelve pages are not distinguished by any special excellence.

Following the twentieth leaf (misplaced as some maintain) are two grants of land, in Irish, for a consideration of three ounces of gold. After these come the Evangelical Symbols again, as reproduced in Plate IV. (fol. 27 V.). The central and some of the other panels in the borders of this page contain miniature work of an astounding perfection.

St. Matthew's portrait with its surrounding border fills the back of *Portrait of* the next leaf (Plate V.). As will be seen in the illustration, the Lion *St. Matthew.* symbol of St. Mark shows its head at each side of the back of the throne ; while the heads of the Calf and Eagle of St. Luke and St. John appear behind the extremities of the seat. The spreading ornaments filling the spandrels of the arch are modelled on the flabellum, an instrument used from an early period in the Eastern Church for the purpose of keeping flies from the altar.

The opening words of St. Matthew's Gospel, " Liber generationis," *The " Liber* one of the most notable instances of illumination in the Manuscript, *generationis"* fill the recto of folio 29 (Plate VI.). The spiral ornamentation and the *page.* general colour harmony of this very beautiful page are particularly striking. Note, too, the curious and rarely relied on effect produced by the alteration of the colours in which the ground and the letters of the word " generationis " are depicted. The rudely-drawn figure standing in the lower left-hand corner is said to represent the Evangelist. The smaller and much more naturally drawn figure at the top may also be intended for him. The difference of execution in the two cases would, I suggest, almost justify the conclusion that the larger figure was a later addition in order to fill a space left vacant when the original artist had touched the Manuscript for the last time. *Its unfinished* I think, too, that we can almost see from the illumination itself the very *condition.* place where he was hurried from his work. There are many unfinished portions in the whole page ; for instance, the small face to the left of the upper limb of the L, the piece of the border of the same limb just above and to the right of the face, and possibly the space into which the right elbow of the upper figure projects. But more noticeable than all these is the unfinished condition of the intertwined letters ER in the circle which forms the lower portion of the antique and curiously formed B. The dark line surrounding the red E is only half completed. The interruption of so very simple a feature of the work seems to tell a tale of perhaps even tragic significance.

The Genealogy of Christ follows, extending to five pages. This *The Genea-* portion of the Manuscript—like the illuminated page just referred to *logy of* and some other pages to be mentioned later—has never been finished. *Christ.* It is nevertheless of extreme interest and great artistic value, as it shows us the very process adopted by the illuminator when at work. Fol. 29 V., for instance, gives us the mere text in two columns with seven finely traced plain circles added by way of incipient ornamentation. In fol. 30 R. we find the same circles filled up in yellow as a ground, one only of them having a slight pattern added in red, while traces of lines are to be seen round parts of the page. The back of this leaf shows the decoration in a further state of advance, corner ornaments of winged bird-like creatures being lightly sketched in in pale mauve and yellow, while some of the central circles are ornamented. A still further advance is disclosed on the page which follows (fol. 31 R.), dots in red being added round a central lozenge, a couple of small illuminated initials being also introduced. There are other instances here and there through the Kells Manuscript of pages being left in an incomplete condition. Obvious examples are to be found in the upper portion of the large L in Plate VI., as already mentioned, and again in Plate VII., where the blank spandrels to right and left of the head of the central figure strike a note of strong discord amidst the colour harmony of their rich surroundings. Again, in the case of the Eusebian Canons, at fol. 4 V., the spandrels of the upper arch have been rudely filled in by some later and very inferior artist ; pale blue triangles, roughly decorated with red, being introduced on a mauve-purple ground, the whole clashing unpleasantly with the extremely fine ornamentation of the remainder of the page.

It is, of course, now impossible to guess with anything approaching certainty how some of the illuminations came to be left unfinished— the death of a great artist before his work was done ; the turmoils and uncertainty of the age ; the necessity for keeping so precious a treasure in concealment when piracy and plunder were always to be feared, will suggest themselves as possibly accounting for these strange lacunæ— but none of these explanations is completely satisfactory. I shall refer to the subject again when dealing with the much disputed question of the actual date of the Manuscript.

The mis-named Doubtful Portrait. The so-called "Doubtful Portrait" on fol. 32 V. (Plate VII.) following the Genealogy is, according to Westwood, "evidently misplaced, and is intended for one of the two Evangelists whose portraits are wanting," that is, St. Mark or St. Luke. The principal figure, as may be seen in the illustration, sits on a chair or throne, and holds a book in the left hand, which is covered by the robe. Westwood here rightly draws attention to the curly flaxen hair, the short stiff beard, the misplaced ears, and the right hand, which appears to be in the act of benediction, with the first and second fingers extended in the Roman manner, the feet evidently wearing sandals, the two peacocks standing on plants in vases, and some other features, which certainly render the picture one of exceptional interest. Gerald Plunket, when the volume was in his possession, had written the words " Jesus Christus " in the blank spandrels to the right and left of the head of the figure. The writing has since been removed, leaving the white spaces somewhat staringly vacant, but no doubt in the very condition they were in when the illumination was interrupted. The presence of the cross above, as the Rev. Mr. Stanford Robinson remarks,* together with the colour of the vestments, the chalice-like cups, the vine, the peacock, and the four angelic beings, most of which are introduced into the decoration of the page, give grounds for Gerald Plunket's ascription. Petrie, too, took the portrait to be that of Christ, and for some reason described the page as " the frontispiece of the Book of Kells." Westwood opposed this view, pointing out, amongst other arguments, that the peacock was occasionally used in early gospels without any suggestion of symbolism. Dr. Abbott, in his " Celtic Ornaments from the Book of Kells," calls it " Portrait of an Evangelist (St. Mark or St. Luke)," but without suggesting any reasons for his description. The title of " Doubtful Portrait " which has clung to the picture so long has in reality no justification whatever ; and some additional and valid reasons, which seem to have been overlooked till now, may be suggested to show that the central figure is intended for either St. Mark or St. Luke, but certainly not for Christ.

The figure on fol. 32 V. (Plate VII.) is obviously one of a series *Portraits of* of four portraits of the Evangelists, which, judging by the surviving *the Gospel* three, are all clearly stamped with a similarity of artistic treatment. *writers.* In each case the Evangelist holds a book in his hand, and occupies a chair or throne in a sitting position. In both Plate V. and VII. the framework surrounding the portrait is identical in the matter of outline of design and general composition. St. John's picture (Plate XVIII.), though its frame differs somewhat from the other two, is, by reason of certain features which are common to all three, sufficiently allied to the others to justify its inclusion in the series. The fact, too, that the head

* " Celtic Illuminated Art," Dublin, 1908.

13

of the latter portrait is surrounded by so magnificent a nimbus, while that of Plate VII. is distinguished by only a very small cross, would seem to preclude the possibility of the latter being intended as a portrait of the Saviour. The presence of the two peacocks, the chalices (if they be such, which is very questionable), and the vine, does not seem to add any great force to the view which Mr. S. Robinson favours, all three being iconographic symbols which are entirely appropriate to the decoration of any portrait of a writer of one of the Gospels. I may also mention that "the four angelic beings" partly relied on by Mr. Robinson consist of two winged figures, and two that are obviously of a human type, and have no wings at all. There is the manifest fact, too, that this page was left in an unfinished state. The spandrels to right and left of the head of the main figure are absolutely blank, and it is to my mind impossible to believe that they were intended to remain so. The borders enclosing the spandrels are also unfinished, as will be seen on comparing them with the same borders lower down. Other evidences of incompleteness will appear on a close study of the exterior corner-pieces of the astoundingly beautiful border. It will be noticed that the interior details of the one at the left top are carried out in every way worthily of the master-hand that did the greater portion of the very intricate patterns with which the page is filled. Look now at the remaining three corner-pieces, and consider the comparatively clumsy and unrefined way in which they are filled in. Although the three are themselves more or less of the same design and colour tone, they are all utterly out of harmony with the first, and form a distinct blot on this most beautifully illuminated page. Look, then, at the four corner-pieces of the consort portrait (Plate V.) and see how harmoniously they are executed, both in colour and design, and it will be at once understood that the three inconsistent and badly-executed corners of Plate VII. must have been left by the greater artist as blank as the spandrel spaces themselves. Further than this, I am strongly inclined to think that the discs which touch the feet of the main figure have also been filled in by the later and inferior artist. A comparison with the similarly situated discs in Plate V., which contain some very fine work, will go far, I think, to justify such a conclusion. The outer trivialities in the way of decoration which are to be seen beyond the corner-pieces in Plate VII., are only too obviously the work of an inferior hand. Is it, then, in all the circumstances conceivable that, if this were a

14

portrait of Christ, it would ever have been left unfinished? Can we imagine that in its manifestly patched condition it would have been used, as Petrie thought it was, as "the frontispiece of the Book of Kells"?

Plate VIII. shows the eight-circled cross, a superb example of the most intricate and delicate ornamentation. It is the only specimen of this type of design in the Kells Manuscript, but it has its counterpart in the Book of Lindisfarne,* the Celtic illuminations of which can alone of all Irish or Anglo-Irish MSS. be compared for beauty, design, or execution, with the pages of the Book of Kells. Westwood thinks that each of the Kells Gospels was preceded by a similarly ornamented leaf, which has disappeared. *The eight-circled cross.*

Facing this eight-circled cross is what is known as the Monogram page (Plate IX.), containing the three opening words of St. Matthew i. 18, "XPI [Christi] autem generatio"—the whole forming, as Professor Westwood rightly remarks, the most elaborate specimen of calligraphy which was perhaps ever executed. The late Rev. Dr. Todd has suggested, with some considerable likelihood, that the ornamental line which runs above the predominant letter is intended to present the usual mark of contraction, placed over the shortened word XPI (Christi). "It may be observed," he adds, "that the page before us contains almost all the varieties of design to be found in Celtic art. These are usually spoken of as twofold: first, arbitrary or geometrical—of which there occur on the page before us the divergent pattern known as the trumpet-pattern, the triquetra, the interlaced curved bands, the knot, and the designs formed of eight lines; secondly, patterns derived from natural forms—foliage, birds, reptiles, fish, quadrupeds, imaginary or monstrous animals, and man." (*Vetusta Monumenta*, Society of Antiquaries, London, 1869). Noticeable amidst such an extraordinary profusion of decorative forms are the three angels to the left, two of whom hold books in one hand and blossom sceptres in the other, the remaining one grasping two of these sceptres—which, in the latter instance, spread into a trefoil pattern. A strange group of animals will be observed between the bottom of the P and the up line of the X—two rats nibbling the Eucharistic bread under the eyes of a pair of cats. The Rev. Mr. Robinson suggests that there may be in this design an allusion to unworthy receivers, and the impending judgment which *The Monogram page.*

* In the Cottonian Library, British Museum.

15

awaited such profanation. Slightly to the right will be seen an otter-like creature with a fish in its mouth. The animal has been described by some critics as rat-like, but its size, shape, and colouring are all against the suggestion. The four diamond panels in the upper portion of the P, which are apparently left plain, are in reality each made up of sixteen small diamond sections most delicately ornamented with key patterns.

Remarks of J. A. Brunn. The observations of J. A. Brunn on this page excellently supplement such quotations as are given above in reference to it :—

"There is a beautiful instance in the book of Kells, presumably surpassing, as a piece of decoration, anything to be met with in any other written book. It is a page to discourage even the most accomplished and most enthusiastic of modern draughtsmen. In nine cases out of ten he will break down before his work is half finished ; or, if he should really succeed in completing it, he will have to expend upon it an amount of time and labour out of all proportion to the apparent result of his work. Mr. Digby Wyatt made an attempt, and had to give it up. Professor J. O. Westwood, who was a great admirer of Irish art and at the same time a skilled draughtsman, went to work with no better result. And he was assuredly not one to be discouraged by difficulties arising from variety of colours and intricacy of design. No one who has had an opportunity of examining the leaves of the big volume containing the Professor's original tracings and now deposited in the Ashmolean Museum at Oxford can have failed to be struck by the minute accuracy of his delineations and the immense pains taken in rendering even the most complicated passages of Celtic ornament. And yet the copying of the monogram page of the Book of Kells was, if not beyond his powers, at least too long and serious an affair to be duly brought to completion. We are indebted to Miss Margaret Stokes, the accomplished writer on Celtic antiques, for possessing at last, a copy* perfectly finished and worthy of an original which the same author, in a brilliant passage referring to its unique variety of design, has signalised as 'an epitome of Irish art.' "†

The text of the Gospel according to St. Matthew follows in large uncial and minuscule combined, initial letters of a highly ornamental

* Now deposited in the National Museum of Ireland, Dublin. A chromo-lithographic reproduction, which, however, is somewhat defective in softness and harmony of colour, may be seen in *Vetusta Monumenta*.

† Margaret Stokes, " Early Christian Art in Ireland," London, 1887, p. 13.

16

character being freely used all through, but without any repetition of design. Other instances of elaborate decoration on a larger scale are furnished later on by a drawing of Christ seized by two Jews (Matthew xxvi. 50) on fol. 114 R., and on the verso of the same leaf the full-page illumination embodying the words "Tunc dicit illis ihs omnes vos scan "[dalum, etc.]. These words have been written in again in a later hand (now a good deal rubbed), as if they had been found difficult to read in their illuminated form.

Plate X., fol. 104 R., furnishes an excellent example of the general *A page of the* run of the written text, with such small illuminated initials and added *text of St.* decorative curiosities as occur so frequently throughout the whole *Mark.* Manuscript. The page is also useful for showing in a brief way the kind of variations from the Vulgate that are to be found everywhere in the Book of Kells. The extract is from Mark xiii. 17–22. The two versions are set side by side for the purpose of convenient comparison :—

BOOK OF KELLS.	VULGATE.
Vae autem praegnantibus Et nutriantibus in illis diebus. Orate autem ut non fiat fuga vestra hime vel sabbato. Erit enim tunc tribulatio magna qualis non fuit ab initio mundi usque modo neque fiet.	*Vae autem praegnantibus et nutrientibus in illis diebus. Orate vero ut hieme non fiant.*
	Erunt enim dies illi tribulationes tales, quales non fuerunt ab initio creaturae, quam condidit Deus usque nunc, neque fient.
*Et nisi braeviati * fuissent dies illi non fieret salva omnis caro sed propter electos braeviabuntur * dies illi. Tunc si quis vobis dixerit ecce hic Christus aut illic nolite credere*	*Et nisi breviasset Dominus dies, non fuisset salva omnis caro : sed propter electos, quos elegit, breviavit dies.*
	Et tunc si quis vobis dixerit, Ecce hic est Christus, ecce illic, ne credideritis.
*Surgent enim saeudo * Christi Et saeudo profetae et dabunt signa magna et prodigia ita in errorem movantur si fieri potest etiam*	*Exurgent enim pseudochristi, et pseudoprophetae, et dabunt signa, et portenta ad seducendos, si fieri potest, etiam electos.*

* The curious arrow-head symbol under the starred words which, as will be seen in the Plate, occurs three times on this page, represents the letter a. It is referred to again in the section dealing with the date of the MS.

The " Tunc crucifixerant" page. Plate XI., fol. 124 R., exhibits the commencement of verse 38 of the 27th chapter of St. Matthew, " Tunc crucifixerant XPI cum eo duos latrones " (" Then were there two thieves crucified with him "). The " XPI," which seems to belong to the sentence, is, as pointed out by Sir John Gilbert, probably only the mediæval note-mark composed of the monogram of " Christi," which was arbitrarily used to call attention to remarkable passages. It was known as the Chrismon. The Vulgate reading of this passage takes a more accurate Latin form in " Tunc crucifixi sunt," this being one of the many differences in reading between that edition and the version contained in the Book of Kells. Reference will be made later on to some more important variations existing between the two texts.

The Evangelical Symbols again occupy a prominent place at the opening of St. Mark's Gospel, fol. 129 V. (Plate XII.), their decorative treatment differing completely from the corresponding page in the previous Gospel. Each of the figures here is furnished with a kind of sceptre. The whole is a most admirably balanced piece of artistic work, both in its decoration and drawing. The misplaced outside central ornament at the bottom is difficult to account for. It possibly represents an attempt to correct by balance the unequal length of the lower limbs of the inverted T panel in the border immediately above. I do not know of any other instance of an error of this kind in the Manuscript.

The " Initium Evangelii " page. The first words of this Gospel, " Initium evangelii Ihu Xpi " (fol. 130 R.), Plate XIII., fill a whole page, the bold magnificence of the three letters INI being especially remarkable. The entire design is filled with the most characteristic details of Celtic ornament, but arranged with extraordinary originality. A studied comparison between it and the " Christi autem generatio," or monogram page (Plate IX.), will show the astounding artistry of both, and at the same time exemplify the wide differences which lie between them The Rev. Mr. Robinson points out the features of the " Initium " design which specially call for notice, and draws attention to " the beautiful effect produced by the interlaced snakes at the four corners of the letter N. The three circles above the letters EVAN are filled with the heads of birds : the other circles above and below are filled with a curious heart-shaped design formed of spirals. The grotesque human figure at the top is held in the grasp of a dragon : under the cross of the T are the wings of two dragons."

With his last sentence I cannot, however, agree, as I fail to see anything grotesque in the figure referred to. It is obviously a holy figure, as shown by the small circles and dots set in triangular groups with which the lower garments are decorated. I shall have some observations later on this very characteristic feature of robe-decoration in the Book of Kells. For the present I suggest strongly that the figure, so far from being grotesque, is intended for the Evangelist St. Mark himself, in just the same way as the other small figures similarly introduced in Plates VI. and XIX. are intended for the respective authors of the illuminated words with which they are surrounded. As to the " dragon," in the grasp of which the figure in Plate XIII. is stated to be held, I do not think it is a dragon. I believe it to be an animal much more appropriate to the surroundings, the symbolical lion of St. Mark himself. A close examination of the plate will show that the saint is assisting the lion in its efforts to devour the red serpent.* The very same contest, omitting the human figure, is depicted in the large illuminated T of the word " Tunc " in Plate XI. The lion's head is the same in both cases, and so are the claws. The claws also correspond exactly with those on the lion in the Evangelical Symbols in Plates IV. and XII. The very unusual form of the G in " Evangelii " should be noticed.

Another full-page illumination (though not amongst those illustrated here) of a strikingly different character of design comes later in the same Gospel, where a tessellated pattern is used with very telling effect. It contains the words of the 25th verse of chapter xv. : " Erat autem hora ter[tia]." The large blank spaces in this page strongly suggest that it was left in an unfinished state. The last page of this Gospel is decorated with two most singular dragon-like monsters, forming lateral diagonal ornaments to the page, an angel and a lion occupying the open side spaces.

St. Luke's Gospel opens with a very striking example of illumination in which the word " Quoniam " fills the whole of fol. 188 R. (Plate XIV.). Some critics, and amongst them Professor Westwood, have suggested that the word is given here in a contracted form, viz., " Qniam " ; but the u and o are both to be seen in the central diamond, the former as a v, and the o as a Greek ω, though somewhat angular in

The " Quoniam " page.

* If a lens is used for the purpose of examining the plates in the present volume it will be found that one of *moderate* capacity is more effectual than a strong magnifier.

19

form. The crowd of figures intermixed with the letters NIAM may possibly have been suggested by the words which follow—" multi conati sunt ordinare narrationem " (" Forasmuch as many have taken in hand," etc.). The trumpet and spiral patterns are here exceptionally fine. The page has been badly mutilated by the former binder both at top and left-hand side. The verso of the leaf contains the words " Fuit in diebus Herodis," which in their simplicity of decoration form a curious contrast to the first word of the Gospel.

The " Qui fuit " pages. Five pages are then occupied with the Genealogy of Christ, each line beginning with " Qui fuit " as illustrated in Plates XV., XVI. and XVII. The initials are all through interlaced with birds, dragons, beasts and snakes. At the bottom of one of these pages (Plate XV.) " is," as Westwood observes,* " an Irish warrior of the sixth century, having in his hand a little round shield (not a long pointed shield like that which the Norman warriors carried, reaching down to their feet) holding a long [?] spear with a spike at the bottom . . . His breeches are prettily ornamented with three spirals, and that is the ordinary way in which the Celtic artists ornamented everything. I know of no other Gospel book which has such a series of letters at the commencement of each portion of the Genealogy, and this is carried on . . . . . . with all that long series of names."

A humorous note. Fol. 201 V. introduces a distinctly humorous note amidst the stained-glass window solemnity attaching to the figure painting of the Manuscript—the same note that is supplied by gargoyles in the architecture of some centuries later. This page of the Genealogy, which in a general way resembles the pages reproduced in Plates XV., XVI. and XVII., contains a string of Q's with which are intertwined a number of droll and impish figures in various grotesque positions, with legs tucked under their arms, and tongues protruding. They pull each other's hair from behind, and one has his toe thrust under the nose of another figure in front. The uppermost of them even carries something resembling the air-bladder of pantomime ; yet all the contortions of their limbs are contrived to fall in with the interlacings of the prevailing scheme of the design, a *tour de force*, as it were, of a big and genuinely human artist in holiday mood after months, or even years, of serious and reverent toil.

A singularly beautiful arabesque, the only example of its kind in

* " The Book of Kells," an Oxford Lecture, 1886.

the Manuscript, fills the middle portion of the fifth of these pages from side to side, forming a terminal to the Genealogy. It is divided into two horizontal panels, the compartment to the right suggesting a vase and vine *motif*, that to the left containing two eagle-headed serpentine creatures whose wings are strangely woven into the general decoration. The whole is surmounted at the centre by the head and shoulders of a human figure wearing a moustache and triple pointed beard, his feet showing below. The entire composition forms one of the most striking instances of lacertine convolution and colour to be found in the volume.

The Temptation of Christ. The controversy of Christ and the Devil (not reproduced) fills fol. 202 V. The drawing here is apparently of a strangely barbarous character; but the draughtsman for all that seems to have been well aware of what was expected of him. The small size of the Devil is obviously intended to convey a suggestion of his powerlessness in the presence of the Saviour. It is noticeable, too, that Satan here has wings but no tail. The figures on the right of Christ are disciples; those above his head, angels. The execution of this page shows also very clearly that more than one artist was engaged on the illumination of the Book of Kells. The better of the two was an incomparable master of his art; the other possessed only very ordinary powers.

The whole-page, "Jesus autem plenus S.S.," which faces the one just mentioned is also of inferior workmanship and design.

Speaking of the Gospels generally, Professor Westwood has drawn attention to an un-Irish usage at the end of the Gospels in the Book of Kells. They do not here conclude with the word "Finit," the words at the end of St. Luke being "Explicit evangelium secundum lucam incipit evangelium secundum johannem." *

St. John's portrait. Fol. 290 R. is occupied by seven widely-spread lines of orange-red minuscule, with some rough attempts at illumination by the introduction of dashes of yellow, mauve, and purple. "Explicit evangelium secundum lucam" is twice repeated, followed by "Incipit evangelium secundum johannem."

Fol. 290 V. shows the Evangelical Symbols again, but in an altered form, at the beginning of St. John's Gospel, the rectilinear frame border being worked into a profusion of decorative interlacements. The following leaf bears the portrait of St. John (Plate XVIII.) with

* Westwood has a misprint here reading "explicit" for "incipit." (*Palæographia Sacra Pictoria.*)

its glorious nimbus. The curious arrangement of the hair is particularly to be noticed, illustrating, as Petrie and others mention, the ancient habit of the Irish. The feet of the figure are enclosed in sandals. More especially deserving of attention are the writing materials with which the Evangelist is furnished. He holds in his hand a long pen, which is shown to be a quill by the feather ending, and at his right foot is a conical ink-pot. I shall have some further observations at a later stage on the writing and writing-materials made use of by the scribes who produced the Manuscript. The so-called "nail" in the right hand of the partially-concealed figure in Plate XVIII. is, I believe, a late addition, and resembles a lighted taper more than anything else. It will be observed that it is held in the hand and not driven through it as a nail would have been.

The "In principio" page. The opening words of St. John's Gospel, "In principio erat Verbum et Verbum" fill the recto of folio 292. Plate XIX. shows the splendidly decorative design into which they are thrown. The four-circle groups forming the terminal ornaments of the IN are instances of the unlimited originality of the artist's decorative skill ; while the extraordinary grace and intricacy of the setting of the letters RINCI are beyond all praise. It is possible that the combination of the C and I is intended to suggest a harper playing a harp : perhaps the fingers of the player, which seem to suggest the harp-strings, may have originated the idea. The figure at the top holding a book is, as in St. Matthew's case (Plate VI.), plainly intended for the author of the Gospel which begins on this page—St. John. The smaller figure, to the right, appears to be raising a conically-shaped cup to his lips.

The missing portions of the MS. The latter portion of this Gospel is wanting. The two closing lines on the recto of the last page (fol. 339) are St. John xvii. 5-6 : "aput te Manifestum nomen tuum hominibus quos dedisti mihi de mundo. Tui." Almost the whole of the text on the reverse side of the leaf has been rendered illegible by attrition—the last surviving words being "Pater sancte" which occur in the eleventh verse of chapter xvii.

No sufficient attention, so far as I am aware, has been drawn to the enormous hiatus in the original Manuscript of which this sudden ending gives a striking proof. No less than four chapters and a half, containing some 152 verses, are missing from the end of St. John, and 52 more from chapters xii. and xiii. A dozen verses are also lacking in St. Luke xii. Having regard to the average number of lines and words contained in each page of the Book of Kells, we find by a simple calculation that at least twenty-four leaves of text alone have disappeared from the book. It is possible, too, that there may have been some full-page illuminations included in the missing portion, so that, allowing an extra leaf for the colophon, and adding a few leaves which are obviously lost at the beginning of the book, together with the missing portrait of one of the Evangelists, we have a total loss of about twenty-nine folios, or fifty-eight pages. All but five of these must have been removed long before the Manuscript came into the hands of Ussher. It is, indeed, more than likely that they had been lost five or six centuries before his time.

The one amongst these many wanted leaves, the loss of which is chiefly to be deplored, is that containing the colophon. It would probably have told when the work was regarded as finished, and might have furnished us with the name of the artist who conceived and wrought the unrivalled wonders of its illuminations.

The royal autographs of Queen Victoria (1849), Prince Albert (1849), and Prince Alfred (1861) are inscribed on one of the supplemental blank leaves at the beginning of the Manuscript. *Royal autographs in the MS.*

Interesting as are the decorative features of the Kells Manuscript, the various readings of the actual text of the Gospels which it contains are of no less interest to students of Biblical history. It should be remembered that Christianity was introduced into Ireland at a very early date ; though it is even now by no means certain whether it reached the country direct from the disciples of Irenæus at Lyons, or from the Roman or English missionaries during an early part of the period in which Great Britain had become a province of Rome. Owing probably to her remoteness from the rest of the civilised world, Ireland retained the primitive religious doctrines and discipline of the Church in their original forms for a much longer time than any other of the West-European communities. Amongst the changes which the Irish Church was slow to recognise was the adoption in the sixth century of St. Jerome's Latin translation of the Bible, commonly called the Vulgate, as the version authorised by the Church of Rome.* The more ancient *The text of the MS.*

* The Golden Gospels, written on purple vellum for Ceolfrid, Abbot of Wearmouth, c. 700, were, as Quaritch states, the first Vulgate text seen in England ("Book Illumination during the Middle Ages," 1889).

Latin version, then displaced, is termed the Old Italic or Ante-Hierony-mian ; and to this version, with occasional modifications, the Irish Church continued to adhere until the beginning of the ninth century. The result was a mixed text, which was used in Ireland for a very considerable time after the adoption of the Vulgate by the authorities at Rome, a very remarkable instance of which mixed version is furnished by the Book of Kells itself—the text of which belongs to the Irish recension of St. Jerome's version.

Its varia-
tions from the
Vulgate.
I have already (page 17 *ante*) illustrated the general nature of the variations between the Kells version and the Vulgate in an extract from St. Mark xiii. They are in the main of a trivial kind and involve no questions of doctrine. In one very important instance, however, there is a much more serious conflict between the two versions, as the following passage from Westwood will show :—

"In the first place I may mention that I detected in it [the Book of Kells] the celebrated passage asserting the divinity of the Holy Ghost, which has hitherto been considered as unique in the Silver Gospels at Vercelli. It occurs in St. John iii. 5, 6 (fol. 297 V.), and is as follows : ' Quod natum est ex carne caro est quia de carne natum est et quod natūm est ex spū (spiritu) sps̄ (spiritus) est quia ds̄ (divinus) sps̄ est et ex dŏ (domino) natus est.' These words were struck out by the Arians, and Father Simon asserted that there was no Latin manuscript in existence in which they were to be found."

There are a considerable number of errors in orthography in the pages of the Irish manuscript, many of which have never been corrected. One important instance of correction is to be found on fol. 219 R., where the text of the preceding page, fol. 218 V., has been erroneously repeated. Attention is drawn to the error by four obeli in red, running down the middle of the page between the lines, and others round the margins, and red lines about the corners. Peculiar spellings of words occur also. Amongst the more notable are " zabulus " and " diabulus " ; " scandalis " for " sandaliis " ; " thensaurus " for " thesaurus " ; " Gychenna " ; " hipochritae " and " chipochritae " ; " cartam " for " quartam," and " beire " for " potum."

The appended table of a few selected variants will show in a very general way how frequently and to what extent the readings of the two versions differ from one another. It will be noticed that whole

24

passages are occasionally included in the Kells Manuscript which are not found in the Vulgate :—

VULGATE.	BOOK OF KELLS.

Caenantibus autem eis accepit Iesus panem et benedixit ac fregit deditque discipulis suis et ait Accipite et comedite ; hoc est Corpus meum.
                              Matth. xxvi. 26.

. . . . . accipit . . . . discipulis suis dicens accipite edite ex hoc omnes hoc est enim Corpus meum quod confringitur pro saeculi vita.

Heli heli lema sabacthani.
                              Ib. xxvii. 46.

Heli heli laba sabacthani.

Ceteri vero dicebant sine videamus an veniat Helias liberans eum.
                              Ib. xxvii. 49.

. . . Helias et liberaret eum. Alius autem accepta lancia pupungit latus ejus et exiit aqua et sangis [sic].

Factum est autem in diebus illis exiit edictum a Caesare Augusto ut describeretur universus orbis.
                              Luke ii. 1.

in illis diebus . . . accessare agusto ut censum profiterentur universi per orbem terrae

ut profiteretur cum Maria desponsata sibi uxore praegnante.
                              Ib. ii. 5.

. . . sibi disponsata . . praegnante de spiritu sancto.

et videbit omnis caro salutare dei.
                              Ib. iii. 6.

et videbitur maies [sic] domini.

genimina viperarum.
                              Ib. iii. 7.

o generatio viperarum.

adveniat regnum tuum : panem nostrum cotidianum da nobis cotidie.
                              Ib. xi. 3.

adveniat regnum tuum : fiat voluntas tua sicut in coelo et in terra, da nobis hodie

[No corresponding passage.] *Ib.* iii. 2 5.	[At end of verse :] *Susciperunt ergo Iesum et portans crucem ducebatur.*
et depositum involvit sindone, et posuit eum in monumento exciso, in quo nondum quisquam positus fuerat. *Ib.* xxiii. 53.	*. . . . in sindone munda . . . . .* *. . . . . . . et imposito eo imposuit monumento lapidem magnam.*
Et cum dixisset, statim discessit ab eo lepra, et mundatus est. *Mark* i. 17	[After *mundatus est*] *et inspiciens Iesus austri vultu eicit eum.*
grex porcorum magnus pascens. *Ib.* v. 11. *et videt tumultum.* *Ib.* v. 38.	*. . . . . . pascensium* [*sic*] *vidit cumuultum* [*sic*].
Et angariaverunt praetereuntem quempiam. *Ib.* xv. 2 1.	*. . . . angarizaverunt . . . .*
Quod natum est ex carne caro est, et quod natum est ex spiritu spiritus est. *John* iii. 6.	*Quod natum est ex carne caro est quia de carne natum est, et quod natum est ex spiritu spiritus est quia deus spiritus est et ex deo natus est.**

The date of the MS.   Of all questions in any way connected with the Book of Kells for which critics have sought a solution, there is none of greater interest than the question of its date. Going, as it does, deep into the mysteries in which the origin and execution of early Irish manuscript illumination have for many centuries been veiled, it has naturally stimulated students of mediæval decorative art to propound at least some theory which

---

* As will be seen, p. 24 *ante*, Westwood misreads the contractions " d̄s̄ " and " d̄ō " as " divinus " and " domino " instead of " deus " and " deo."

would fix within a century or two the period in which so perfect an example of miniature ornament can have been produced. Indications to suggest its time of birth have been sought in all possible directions. Historical evidence is of little assistance. The Manuscript itself fails us where, conceivably, it might have helped us most, for the page that should have told its story is unfortunately no longer there. The style of its writing, the particular version of the Scriptures it contains, the nature of its decorative embellishments, its orthography, pigments, ink, and even the manner in which its vellum was prepared, have one and all engaged the close attention of those who know much on all these matters ; yet in spite of all that has been written on the subject, no one can say with any certainty to-day whether it belongs to the sixth or the ninth century. The early commentators on the Manuscript ascribe it without hesitation to the sixth century, O'Donovan and Dr. Todd being amongst them. Miss Stokes and Professor Middleton say it belongs to the latter half of the seventh century, and in agreement with them are Westwood and Sir E. M. Thompson. The Rev. Mr. Stanford Robinson, relying largely on a comparison of its text and ornamentation with those of the Book of Durrow, thinks it cannot be placed earlier than the eighth century ; while Dr. T. K. Abbott assigns it to that century also. Dr. E. H. Zimmermann, in the Prospectus of a comprehensive work which was in preparation in 1914, "Die Vorkarolingischen Minia-turen," dates the Kells Manuscript c. A.D. 700, making it more or less contemporary with the Book of Durrow. A study of the initials of the latter Manuscript satisfies him that *its* date is about a century later than usually believed. Sir John Gilbert gives it any time between A.D. 600 and 900 ; while Brunn holds that it was produced in the ninth century under the influence of the early renaissance in the reign of Charlemagne. The latest view expressed on the subject is that of Mr. R. A. S. Macalister ("Essays and Studies," 1913), who seeks to show that the Book of Lindisfarne—which he suggests, and most people believe, was earlier than the Kells Manuscript—belongs to the ninth century, c. 830. This would place the Kells volume about the middle of the same century.

The cause of this very wide disagreement is no doubt in the main attributable to the small number of similarly decorated works which are now available for comparison. Brunn is very nearly correct when he states that foliageous ornament is absent in the earlier period of Irish

27

illumination,* but he has only the few surviving specimens on which to base his judgment. Hundreds of fine manuscripts must have been carried off, burnt, or otherwise destroyed when the Northmen were ravaging Ireland ; and it is quite possible that many of those which perished did not conform to Brunn's views as to the absence of phyllomorphic forms. We do know that the Kells Manuscript is full of foliageous forms such as the trefoil and the vine, not to instance others, and that the manuscript which is alone comparable with it in decoration, the Book of Lindisfarne, is practically without them. In the circumstances we must be content to leave the matter in uncertainty, although there is no proof before us that a thorough analytical examination has ever been made by anyone of *all* the manuscripts of the Irish school both at home and abroad.

There is one fact connected with the Book of Kells on which an argument—though not a very strong one—might be founded in support of the later date theory. As previously mentioned, the Manuscript is in a good many of its decorative portions unfinished. It is now certain that some at least of the unfinished ornaments have been continued by an inferior hand. The " Annals of the Four Masters " give us the names of no less than sixty-one remarkable scribes who flourished in Ireland before the year 900, forty of whom lived between A.D. 700 and 800. The art of illumination seems to have deteriorated rapidly in Ireland after about A.D. 900. Now, if the original artist of the Kells Manuscript had almost completed his work at an early date, say between 650 and 750, there would have been roughly a couple of centuries during which the services of one of these " remarkable scribes " would have been available for the completion of the comparatively small portion left unfinished. Even if originally produced in the year 800, there would have been still one hundred years in which to get a first-class artist to fill the gaps. It is a matter of some difficulty to believe that there *were* such opportunities of completing the volume in a manner worthy of its original condition, and that they were neglected. It is, on the other hand, very easy to see, if the first miniaturist had left his work unfinished, say, late in the ninth century, that there would then have been little chance of procuring the services of an artist equal to

* Miss Stokes, too, is quite emphatic in reference to the Book of Durrow, which is admittedly one of the earliest Irish manuscripts : " There is no sign of any vegetable forms being used." Yet the illustration she gives, from the Book of Durrow ("Early Christian Art in Ireland," p. 17), seems to throw some doubt upon her assertion.

the first. The fact that an inferior hand has too frequently left his mark upon the decorations of this splendid Manuscript cannot, for the reasons mentioned, do anything to help the cause of those who favour an early date.

One other, now well recognised, method of determining (at least *Contraction* approximately) the date of an early manuscript has not been syste- *marks used* matically applied to the Book of Kells. Professor Lindsay and the *in the MS.* Palæographical Society have in recent years done excellent work of a general kind in connection with the subject of contractions in Latin manuscripts, but Ludwig Traube has been the first of our latest commentators to formulate anything in the nature of a law bearing on the date values to be extracted from such shortened forms as are found in early writings. In the case of the word *noster* he has conclusively shown* that the forms n̄i, n̄o, and n̄m (short for nostri, nostro, and nostrum) were introduced in the sixth century and predominated in the seventh and eighth ; while the forms n̄ri, n̄ro, and n̄rm appear in the eighth century and predominate in the ninth ; and it is largely by the application of this law that the New Palæographical Society fix the date of the British Museum manuscript " Liturgical Prayers " (" Facsimiles," Pl. 132, Part VI.). It is true that the large and bold character of the Kells script does not lend itself much to contraction except in the case of holy words, such as IHS for Jesus, ds for deus, sp̄s for spiritus, and other usual shortenings ; but there are occasional instances of another kind. The letters ae, for example, are now and then abbreviated into ę, a form of contraction that will be found three times on the page set out in Plate X. and once in Plate XV. (Mathathię). It is true that this abbreviation occurs in other Irish manuscripts of an early date ; but there is a variant of it in the Kells Manuscript which does not seem to have been observed, and one which I have not succeeded in finding elsewhere, viz., â, in which the single-barbed arrow *above* the letter represents the e of the diphthong. It occurs, for instance, in fol. 124 V., where " vae " is written " uâ," and it will be seen in Plate XVI., though in a slightly different position, in connection with the word " ressa " = ressæ. Similarly, in Plate XV. " ianne " with same mark to right of the e = " iannæ."† The fact that this variant is a refinement, as it were,

* *Nomina Sacra.* München, 1907.
If it be objected that the arrow in the last two cases is a flourish and not a contraction mark, I would draw attention to the fact that the flourishes here are *attached* to the letter, while contraction marks are *detached*.

29

of the other abbreviation of ae, strongly suggests that its use indicates a later date. The matter would seem to be worthy of further palæographical study.

The ornamentation of the robes.

I have already alluded to a very characteristic form of ornamentation which is found on many of the robes depicted in the Manuscript, or in their immediate neighbourhood in the full-page illuminations, namely the dots, or small circles, in triangular groups. I find no reference to this feature in any of the writings on the Book of Kells, although the consistency with which it manifests itself seems to be full of strong suggestion. If, for obvious reasons, we except three Plates, viz., VIII., XI., and XIV., all the full-page illuminations reproduced here will be found to contain instances of its occurrence. The triangle was, as we know, symbolical of the Trinity, and so of Christianity generally, in mediæval times. For this reason perhaps it is that its use in the Book of Kells is confined to the garments, symbols, or surroundings of only holy personages. It is not found, for instance, on the garments of the two Jews in the picture of the arrest of Christ ; nor does it appear in connection with the six small half-figures in the border panel of Plate II., all of whom have their backs turned to the Virgin and Child. Its occurrence may therefore be taken to indicate a badge of association with Christ and His teaching : its absence, to denote an anti-Christian attitude, unless there be present some other unmistakable mark of holiness such as wings, book, or blossom-sceptre. I cannot help thinking that an exhaustive investigation of other illuminated manuscripts would produce some new and valuable evidence, arising from the use or the absence of this symbolic ornament, on the question of the date of the Kells Gospels. To what country or school of ornamentation it owes its origin it is at present impossible to say. It does not seem to have been the result of Byzantine influences, for, as a matter of fact, there are no traces of its use in the Book of Lindisfarne, the figure miniatures of which are more Byzantine in their character than those of any other Celtic manuscript. So far as I am aware there is no clear instance of its use in manuscripts of the Irish School at home or abroad before the ninth century ; and although it may occasionally be seen in that century in both Celtic and Carolingian illuminations, I have found no such restrictive conditions attaching to its employment as are manifestly observed in its use in the Book of Kells. If this view be undisputed, I can only conclude that we have here yet another fairly

30

reliable proof that the Book of Kells itself cannot have been earlier than the year 800—in other words, that it is a ninth-century manuscript.

The actual writing of the Book of Kells is in itself the embodiment *The hand-* of an early Irish School of calligraphy, which sprang into being in *writing in the* circumstances for which it would be difficult to find a parallel in the *MS.* history of handwriting in any part of the world. It is acknowledged on all sides that before the arrival of St. Patrick in about the year 430, the inhabitants of Ireland were all but destitute of a written literature of any kind. Christianity had undoubtedly made some little way amongst the people before the landing of Patrick, and possibly a few Latin manuscripts may have been used in the service of the earliest missionaries in Ireland. In the written Irish language we have no work surviving, excepting the Book of Armagh, of an earlier date than A.D. 1100.

St. Patrick too often has been described as being a single pioneer *St. Patrick's* of Christianity. He was in reality, as we now know, attended by a *interest in* large and well-equipped company of earnest workers, carrying with *letters.* them no small quantity of literary material. If we can accept the Book of Armagh as an authority to be relied on, the missionary party that accompanied St. Patrick included some artists. The holy Bishop Assicus was one of them—and is described as Patrick's worker in brass, who was wont to make altars and book-caskets. The same authority tells us that Patrick carried with him to the other side of the Shannon a large number of bells, patens, chalices, altars, law-books and Gospels for use in the churches founded there. Next after his conversion of the Irish Kings, Druids and people, the Saint's greatest achievement was the introduction of the Latin tongue and his making it the ecclesiastical language of Ireland. Tradition tells us, too, that he used himself to write alphabets for young men who were chosen for a clerical career. It is here that his immediate connection with the Book of Kells becomes apparent ; and it is to him, helped by the artistic taste of the schools of Irish penmanship that came after his date, that we are indebted for the striking and always graceful handwriting which is so strong a characteristic of all the early manuscripts of Ireland, and not least of the Gospels of Colum Cille. The most remarkable feature of this fine type of writing is that, excepting the fact that it developed in Ireland, there is nothing whatever Irish about it. The models employed for the individual letters were purely Roman—the half-uncial forms largely used at the time in Franco-Lombardic and other such manuscripts of Western Europe. But, as Sir Edward M. Thompson tells us (" Greek and Latin Palæography "), " having once obtained their models, the Irish scribes developed their own style of writing and went on practising it, generation after generation, with astonishing uniformity. The English conquest did not disturb their even course. The invaders concerned themselves not with the language and literature of the country. They were content to use their own style of writing for grants of land and other official deeds ; but they left it to the Irish scribes to produce manuscripts in the native characters."

It is manifest that the high degree of cultivation attained by Irish calligraphy " did not result," as Dr. F. Keller puts it, " from the genius of single individuals, but from the emulation of numerous schools of writing, and the improvements of several generations. There is not a single letter in the entire alphabet which does not give evidence, both in its general form and its minuter parts, of the sound judgment and taste of the penman." (" Ulster Journ. Archæology," viii. 223.) In the hand in which the Book of Kells is mainly penned there are occasional deviations from the standard forms of the Roman half-uncial letters. Two forms of S, for instance, are used, the round capital and the tall half-uncial. A preference is also shown for the capital R—obviously for greater clearness. Three forms of " a " are used ; " b " and " l " are always bent ; " d " is both with the perpendicular stroke (d) and with the stroke thrown back (ð).* Other peculiarities may be noticed in the Plates of the text.

More than one hand in the script. It may here be mentioned that (as in the case of the illuminations) more than one hand was at work on the script. In addition to the round half-uncial form in which the greater portion of the Book of Kells is written, there are very distinct traces of the handwriting of two other scribes. In one of the folios is an example, as pointed out in the Introduction to Bond and Thomson's " Facsimiles of Manuscripts " (The Palæographical Society, 1873–1883). Here the whole page, excepting the last line, " is transitional, and goes a step nearer to a minuscule form of writing, the letters being thinner in stroke and more compressed ; the second, exhibited in the last line, is entirely minuscule, and of the character called pointed. This pointed hand

* Examples of almost all these forms are to be seen in the text reproduced in Plate X. See p. 17 *ante* for an uncontracted reading of the whole.

became the ordinary cursive hand of the Irish, which has lasted to the present day."

The most curious fact connected with the extraordinary adoption by Ireland of the letters of another country is that, although it was at the time merely for the purpose of writing Latin, or the language of the Church, the nation that effected the appropriation has continued from then down to the present to employ, with one or two exceptions, these same Roman letters in the writing of the old Irish language.

The Irish monks not only perfected this script in their native schools, *The Irish* but they carried it with them when any of them left Ireland on their *hand abroad.* many missions for the propagation of the Christian faith abroad—first to Iona, and from thence to Northumbria, and the South of England, and so on to almost every part of Europe. A very early instance of the effect produced abroad by the Irish is furnished by a manuscript now in St. Peter's, Rome, " S. Hilarius on the Trinity," the date of which is well established as A.D. 496–523. The writing is described by the editors of the Palæographical Society's " Facsimiles " as " early minuscule, showing Irish influence . . . the manuscript itself may have been written in Italy, in a monastery where Irish influence was predominant." Sir Edward M. Thompson acknowledges that England was almost entirely indebted to Ireland for her national handwriting. Miss Stokes, Dr. Keller, and others have well described the widespread operations of the Irish monks abroad, the monasteries they founded, the libraries they furnished with works of their own hands, written and illuminated in a fashion similar to that of the Book of Kells.

All writers on mediæval palæography acknowledge the importance of the Celtic tradition as an influence on the decorative forms of Continental illuminated manuscripts ; but it should not be forgotten that the Byzantine school of illumination, with its stern and mosaic-like formality, had been moving steadily westward from very early days in the Christian Era. The Book of Lindisfarne (A.D. 800–825) is an instance, with its figures and draperies strongly impressed with traces of Eastern tradition. Italy and France had at an even earlier date been largely affected by the same artistic pressure. The antagonism between the Byzantine and the Celtic ideas of decoration lasted, indeed, for many centuries, each school all the time losing something of its own, and absorbing something in return from the traditions of its opponent. Something approaching a fusion of the two was brought

33

about in a new style of decoration which originated in France under the encouragement of Charlemagne towards the close of the eighth century, and the artistic revival which followed, and spread through Western Europe as far as the South of England, may be said to have shaped the spirit and the form of all European pre-Gothic art. Some centuries later the complete interfusion of these clashing traditions resulted in the development of an entirely new type of manuscript illumination both in France and England. Two superb examples of such work, dating from early in the fourteenth century, were presented to the nation within the last two years by Mr. H. Yates Thompson, the well-known collector of illuminated manuscripts and books ; one of them, the St. Omer Psalter, representing the union of the contending schools in their highest state of development in East Anglia, the other, the Metz Pontifical, embodying, though in a less marked degree than the other volume, the amalgamation of Byzantine and Celtic decorative traditions at the top of its perfection in France. Curiously enough, the latter manuscript shares with the Book of Kells the misfortune of having been left unfinished, and the cause of its being so can only be guessed at. Some of its uncompleted pages, however, teach us a good deal as to the actual process of its illumination, a compensation also furnished by the uncompleted portions of the Kells volume. The fuller story of the general influence of the Celtic style of ornament, its spreading, its commingling with decorative forms abroad, and its decline, interesting though it all may be, is outside the purpose of this Introduction.

The pens of the Irish scribes. Returning to the subject of the writing of the Kells Manuscript, we find that differing views have been entertained as to the writing instruments used by the Irish scribes, many palæographers believing that the marked neatness and firmness of the handwriting can only be attributed to the employment of extremely sharp metallic pens or reeds. Amongst the first to reject this belief was Dr. Keller, whose opinion—now very generally accepted—was that the early Irish pens were the quills of swans, geese, crows, and other birds. The representation of St. John in the Book of Kells (Plate XVIII.) and some other more or less contemporary pictures from ancient manuscripts were rightly relied on by him in support of his contention. The early monkish inkpot is also illustrated in the last-mentioned Plate : it was usually conical in shape, and attached either to the arm of the scribe's chair, or fastened to a stick let into the floor. The vellum, or parchment,

34

used by the Irish scribes is generally much thicker than that used by *The vellum* the French from the seventh to the tenth century—the leaves of the *and the ink.* Book of Kells are no exception. It is at times finely polished, but more often it is hard and not well cleaned. Goats, sheep, and calves supplied the skins, but the Irish preparation of them was by no means the best.

The blackness of their ancient ink, even at the present, is quite remarkable. It has been found to resist the action of chemical tests of iron, seeming to be composed of materials not generally used in ink making.

In the matter of its punctuation, the written text of the Book of *The punctua-* Kells is not a very good example of the Irish practice as described by *tion of the MS.* Dr. F. Keller. Speaking of the early Irish manuscripts generally, he tells us that three dots (∵) mark a period; two dots, a comma ; (..,), a semicolon ; and one dot at half the height of the letters, a comma. It is true that instances of the practice may be seen in the present Plates and elsewhere in the Manuscript, but there does not appear to be any-thing like the uniformity observed throughout which Dr. Keller mentions. The subject, in truth, is one that is only now beginning to be studied with such closeness as is required before we can lay down any really comprehensive rules governing the use of stops by the scribes of early Irish manuscripts. We find, as a fact, in the Book of Kells, many consecutive lines, embracing two or three fully completed sentences, where there is no trace of punctuation at all. The period, or full stop, is variously represented : (1) by three dots (∵); (2) by one dot at half the height of the letter ; (3) by omitting the punctuation mark altogether and beginning the next sentence with a striking illuminated initial. So common, indeed, is this last form in the Kells text, that one wonders why full stops should ever be introduced before so obvious an indication of a new sentence as is provided by these fine and con-stantly recurring initials. Occasionally also the very size of the initial tells a reader the value of the stop—as, for instance, where a half-height dot is followed by a small initial, one knows it is something in the nature of a comma. The half-height dot is also used to mark the commence-ment of a speech, as a colon is commonly used to-day.

Another point connected with the punctuation found in the Kells *The stops* Manuscript has, so far as I am aware, been overlooked by all palæo- *square in* graphers. None of them seems to have noticed that the dots of which *shape.*

35

the punctuation is formed are, in the Kells volume, almost always square in shape, or quadrilateral—not round. In itself it would seem to be a matter of little moment ; and one might easily jump to the conclusion that this particular shape was employed as best suited to fit in with the type of letters used. There may, however, be a deeper meaning attached to it, and one possibly capable of throwing some light on the question of the date of the Manuscript. A cursory examination of such reproductions of Latin script as are set out in Sir Edward M. Thompson's admirable book, " Greek and Latin Palæography," the " Facsimiles " of the Palæographical Society, and some other works of a similar nature that I have consulted, shows with considerable clearness that the square form of punctuation marks does not seem to have been common until about the tenth century. Traces of its use are no doubt to be met with in one or two manuscripts supposed to be of an earlier date ; but there will, I think, be found after the tenth century and on to the twelfth a very striking consistency in the use of square, and not round punctuation. In no other manuscript or reproduction that I have seen are there such clear-cut, square-shaped stops as in the Book of Kells. I would suggest, though with much diffidence, that as in the case of musical notation, where the earlier square form gave place, at a more or less definite date, to the round form now almost universally made use of, so here may perhaps be found an additional argument for ascribing a later date to the Book of Kells than that assumed by the majority of students.

The ornamentation of the MS.

The ornamentation of the Book of Kells when broken up into its component parts will be found to be made up of four main divisions. The same, if we except phyllomorphic forms, may be said of nearly all the other decorated manuscripts produced in or about the same period :—

1. Patterns in the composition of which geometrical combinations or developments of straight or curved lines form the sole element, viz., the spiral and the interlacing.
2. Zoomorphic, or animal forms.
3. Phyllomorphic, or leaf and plant forms: the two last-named classes being motives of a conventionalised kind, which though unnatural in treatment are derived from nature.
4. Figure representations.

36

A good deal has been written on the three less important divisions of decorative types—I shall return to them later—but of infinitely greater interest are the sub-divisions of the first class which embody all that can be described as Celtic art in its most characteristic expressions, the spiral and the interlacement—and which, singly or in combination, are woven with such unerring taste into the decorative texture of the Book of Kells. With the origin of these is involved the story of pre-historic national art tendencies which go back into the mists of long-forgotten ages. Their very existence in far-away times can only be surmised ; their developments can only be extracted as it were by a process of spectrum analysis from the converging rays of a remote antiquity which are gathered into focus in the illumination of such a volume as the Gospels of Colum Cille and other works of a similarly decorative type. In truth, underlying these two apparently simple forms of design is a racial romance, which commences with the earliest origin of the Indo-European immigration, and continues through thousands of years, and in ever-shifting changes of scene, down to the time at which the westward-tending multitudes began to settle in Ireland and form what has since been known as the early Irish people.

The trumpet pattern, or divergent spiral, as will be seen in many *The spiral* of the Plates, is composed of two winding lines which afterwards diverge *pattern.* into a trumpet form, the open end of which is closed by a curved line. A new spiral springs in inverted order from the points of the curved line—the two winding lines repeating the original pattern in converging directions until they reach a central point. Then they start again, diverging and converging as before in an almost infinite succession of spiral forms. In its earliest type, as found in the great tumuli of the New Grange Group (c. 1200 B.C.), and later between 200 B.C. and A.D. 200 on metal ornaments, the curve is large and simple ; in Christian times the curved spaces were treated as secondary to the spiral and the turns round the central point are frequently twelve or more. After the tenth, and perhaps the beginning of the eleventh century, this design seems to have dropped out of Irish art. As a form of simple decoration its origin is possibly coeval with the earliest efforts of the most archaic civilisation. In pre-Hellenic ages, about 2200 B.C., it was already well known in Crete, as shown by the Kamares vases found within the last fourteen years in the now excavated Palace of Phaestos. From thence it passed to Egypt and Mycenæ. The wandering races, whether Tuatha

37

da Danaan, Firbolgs, Celts, or Milesians that ultimately reached and settled in Ireland, had, on their way west from Scythia and the Ægean, been in touch with many forms of civilisation. Those of them that took the South European route dwelt long in Egypt, Greece, Crete, Italy, and Spain; those that took a more northerly and transalpine way had, under the name of Celtae, occupied all central Gaul; while others of them spread through North-west Europe, making their chief seat in Scandinavia. Each succeeding wave brought its own types of ornament, tribal or national as the case might be, changed perhaps in trivial respects from what they were originally, but sufficiently characteristic to form the basis of higher artistic developments when occasion arose for putting them to use.*

J. A. Brunn's views. In the words of Johan A. Brunn,† whose name I have already mentioned : " The spiral design was no accidental feature in the pages of Celtic art, nor was it confined to such simple, uniform scrolls as those we find used as a kind of border ornament by several prehistoric peoples. It was, on the contrary, a favourite pattern of a very elaborate character, applied as a surface decoration to a variety of objects, such as shields, helmets, sword sheaths, armlets, horse-trappings, and personal ornaments, examples of which still survive, testifying to an astonishing proficiency in metal work—bronze and gold—both as regards construction and decoration.

" It has been suggested that, at least in some types, it was developed under the influence of floral or foliated schemes transplanted from classical ground.‡ If so that might account for part of its force and freedom, qualities so rare in an ornament of purely geometrical extraction ; while, on the other hand, in case the opinion be correct, the Celtic pattern may be said to be the most ingenious translation ever made of

* Mr. George Coffey (" The Bronze Age in Ireland," 1913) writes : " Ireland during the Bronze Age was not isolated, but stood in direct communication with the Continent. Ægean and Scandinavian influences can be detected in the great tumuli of the New Grange Group, and Iberian influence is discernible in some of the later types of bronze implements. Ireland . . . was during the Bronze Age a kind of western El Dorado, owing to her great richness in gold." Mr. Coffey assumes that spirals were introduced from Scandinavia, where this motive had penetrated early from the Ægean along the amber route.

† " An Enquiry into the Art of the Illuminated MSS. of the Middle Ages." Stockholm, 1897.

‡ Mr. George Coffey, for instance, thinks that Celtic designs were (after 400 B.C.) influenced by classical anthemion and meander patterns, which were modified by the Celtic love of spiral and scroll.

38

a foliageous design into a geometrical one. One might think of its being introduced together with the stock of ornaments brought from other countries by the early Christian missionaries. But it would be very difficult, if not impossible, to point to a single scheme in decorative art outside of the Celtic area with greater claim than the so-called late Celtic to be considered as the prototype that suggested the spiral design shown in manuscripts and other works of the Christian era."

The second subdivision of the main or first class type, the interlace- *The inter-* ment pattern, is also well described by Brunn :— *laced pattern.*

" This type of pattern may be characterised as a surface decoration composed of one or more ribbons or straps of uniform size, which are twisted, plaited, knotted, or otherwise interwoven so as to cover the field with a symmetrically disposed design. It occurs in a variety of forms, from the plain twist, or guilloche, to the elaborate chain composed of knots of torturing intricacy and of varied construction, being laid in squares, circles, oblongs, triangles, hexagons, octagons, etc. The more intricate forms are predominant ; and, by variety of design and the unerring precision with which the ribbons are interwoven so as to cross over and under alternately and finally be joined up to each other, testify to the astonishing capacity of the draughtsman. When compared with the spiral ornament, the interlaced work looks rather mechanical. . . . Hence it came that these held a very subordinate place to the more complicated patterns. An interlaced series would receive an additional enrichment in various ways."

The immediate origin of this universally characteristic feature of Celtic illumination is in all probability to be found in decorative remains of North Italy and Southern Gaul dating from the second and third centuries. It did not become widely popular in Irish Art until the seventh century.

Amongst other geometrical motives of which the first division is *Fret and dia-* composed, should be included the fret pattern, which is employed in *per patterns.* a considerable number of forms as a filling for panels in both borders and initials. The peculiarity of the Celtic fret, which is strongly distinguished from the square type so usual in Greek art, lies in the bending of the links, at certain points, at angles of 45° instead of 90°. The whole assumes in this way a peculiar Chinese character.

Diaper work is occasionally introduced to brighten small spaces lying between the larger designs of more extended elaboration. It occurs in the Book of Kells in many varieties, and in conjunction with rosettes, a detail of ornamentation somewhat foreign to Celtic art.

Dotted patterns.   Dots, too, mostly red in colour, are one of the leading features of the less important details of decoration. They are often used by themselves to form patterns in extended lines for filling vacant spaces in a large design, as in the Book of Lindisfarne. Their more usual employment in the Book of Kells is for the purpose of adding as it were a fringe to exterior lines. Their use is very frequently relied on in the case of the smaller initials. (*See* Plates XX to XXIV)

A somewhat curious distinction, in relation to this type of ornamentation, is to be found between the Book of Kells and the Lindisfarne Gospels. In the former the dots are almost always in single lines, while in the latter they are frequently used in double lines, producing a somewhat richer form of fringe.*

Plant forms of decoration.   In the matter of phyllomorphic forms the decoration of the Book of Kells presents a remarkable contrast to nearly all the early Irish illuminated manuscripts. J. A. Brunn goes so far as to say : " Foliageous ornament is entirely unknown in the Celtic illuminated manuscripts of the earlier period." The presence of these forms here will be obvious to any observer of the details of the Plates reproduced in this volume. Their introduction is in many respects, however, extremely difficult to account for. Brunn has well described what he styles this " most important innovation," but without drawing any definite conclusion as to the exact meaning of its first appearance in this Manuscript :—

" The element appears, to begin with, among the flourishes and terminals, in the shape of lightly-sketched branches with leaves and flowers, sometimes proceeding from vases. Of a more elaborate nature are the scrolls of foliage which are seen to fill in, as a surface decoration, long, narrow borders or panels in the grand illuminated pages. The most characteristic form is a pattern of a single wavy stem with alternate recurved scrolls terminating in trefoil-shaped leaves. Also in this position the stem is occasionally found to proceed from a vase. More general, however, is a less rational connection of leaf design with zoo-

* The double rows of red dots are also found in MacDurnan's Gospels (Lambeth Palace Library), but this manuscript is not regarded as earlier than the end of the ninth century.

morphic patterns. Thus a branch of foliage is frequently seen to evolve from between the open jaws of a nondescript, while at the same time the tail of the beast presents the appearance of a trefoil or lance-shaped leaf. And there are other patterns in which zoomorphic forms are intertwined with undulating stems of foliage, much on the same principle as the compositions which, in the previous pages, we have observed in dialects of non-Celtic decorative art."

The fact stated by Brunn, like all statements of fact regarding the Irish illuminations, is of course based only on the evidence supplied by the still surviving examples of such work. It is, no doubt, within the bounds of possibility that some strange and accidental recovery of other examples of the many manuscripts which have disappeared long ago might upset any theories formed on the decorative features of those which we actually possess ; but until such recovery be made it seems rational to assume that the subsisting specimens represent the average character of those which have perished. But here is the difficulty if we act on this assumption. The majority of palæographers put the date of the Book of Kells as not later than the eighth century. Do any of this majority allow that leaf or plant forms of decoration are found so early in other existing Celtic manuscripts ? If not, the Kells Manuscript, although confessed by all to have reached the high-level mark in Irish illumination, occupies a strangely isolated position in the Celtic schools of decoration, where it never inspired even a single scribe to imitate in other works the effects produced by its artistic introduction of new foliageous forms. If, on the other hand, the date of the Kells Gospels be brought down to the ninth century or later, the innovation of its leaf and plant ornamentation ceases to be striking, and fits in with what most critics allow to be the case ; as well as smoothing over some other incongruities (already referred to) which are inseparable from any theory of an earlier production.

No account that might be written of the zoomorphic, or animal, *Zoomorphic* forms introduced in the decoration of the Manuscript could convey any *decoration.* impression of a more effective kind than that given by the plates themselves. At the same time it is well to bear in mind that the true explanation of their unnatural drawing is not to be attributed to the incapacity of the artist. Such deviations from nature as they exhibit are due more or less to the same causes that led to the eccentricities attaching to the human figures represented : in other words, there never was any intention on the artist's part to depict these animal forms in their natural shapes. Whatever they happen to be, fish, peacock, horse, dog, hare, otter, cat, rat, cock, lizard, serpent, or dragon, they are all in a sense creatures of a world apart, strongly marked with the deliberate unreality of ecclesiastical heraldry ; distant relations, as it were, of the lion, the calf, and the eagle, of the Evangelical symbols, and forced into disnatured anatomies and fantastic posturings only to serve the purposes of the artist, and fall in with the general decorative scheme of which they form a symmetrical part. In this way only, according to the tenets of the early Irish School of illumination, could artistic harmony be preserved ; and curious as such living forms may be when contrasted with the more correct and altogether natural pictures of animal life in the Continental manuscripts of a later day, it can at least be said that, as compared with the strange creatures we have been long familiar with in heraldry, the fauna of the Book of Kells are not much more extravagant than the singular creatures that owe their origin to the Heralds' College.

Serpentine decoration. The frequently recurring presence of serpentine forms all through the decorations of the Manuscript has given rise to the suggestion that these forms are in some way connected with the worship of ophidian reptiles. There certainly appears to be some evidence to show that amongst the mmigrant races that had established themselves in the land before the introduction of Christianity the worship of the serpent was practised, though perhaps not very widely. It is even possible that this was the serpent which St. Patrick is said to have driven out of the country. The adoption of this serpentine form by the Church for decorative purposes would have been but another instance of what we know was the custom of the Christian Church in very early days, when many pagan elements were for good reasons absorbed into the practices of the Christian missionaries, and afterwards became permanently interwoven with Christian belief. Both St. Jerome and St. Augustine strongly upheld this course of action on grounds of expediency when dealing with converts from paganism.

Dr. F. Keller, writing of Irish early ornament generally, says :—

" In all these ornaments there breathes a peculiar spirit, which is foreign to the people of the West : there is in them a something mysterious which imparts to the eye a certain feeling of uneasiness and suspense. This is especially the case with those frightful-looking, monstrous figures of animals, whose limbs twist and twine themselves into a labyrinth of ornaments, where one can hardly resist the natural impulse to search for the other parts of their bodies, often nearly concealed or passing into different strange creatures . . . The variety of these forms . . . their luxuriant development, often extravagant, but sometimes uncommonly delicate and lovely . . . must have been originated in the East, or at least have their prototypes there. That the Irish system of ornamentation does actually find an analogy in Eastern countries is proved by the illustrations published by C. Knight in a small work on Egypt. We find there the serpentine bands of the Irish ornaments appearing already in the oldest Egyptian and Ethiopian manuscripts, and with a similarity of colour and combination truly astonishing."

When we come to consider the fourth division of the ornamentation of the Manuscript, it may be said that, among the many strange features of this remarkable volume, there is none stranger than the representation it gives us of the human figure. Such adjectives as " barbaric," " grotesque," " distressing," " hideous," with others of a like kind, are commonly used by writers when referring to them ; and suggestions are boldly put forward to the effect that in spite of all their capability for decoration of the highest kind, the hands that framed, and the minds that conceived the ornamental pages of this very marvellous work were unable to present either human or super-human faces, their anatomy, or their garments, in any other but the apparently inadequate form in which such drawings have been made. Ruskin's words on this subject are : " The Celts developing peculiar gifts in linear design, but wholly incapable of drawing animals or figures " (" The Pleasures of England ") —a comment based upon an obviously superficial knowledge of the aims of the Irish illuminators. Byzantine influences are strongly relied on by some high authorities as being the controlling lead that shaped their eccentricities, and even relied on by such of them as deny the possibility of Byzantium having had anything to do with the purely ornamental accessories which surround these very figure drawings. *Figure paint-ing in the MS.*

43

That extremely intelligent writer on Celtic illumination, Johan A. Brunn, expresses his views on the subject in the work already cited thus :—

"It may be that this very imperfect style of draughtsmanship, which appears to modern onlookers so ridiculously childish and grotesque, was viewed by its contemporaries with a very different eye from that with which a modern critic views the same thing. It may be that the absurdities in form and colour, which make the figures of the Saviour and His Apostles appear to us like so many rudely expressed travesties, were veiled by a sentiment similar to that which makes the pious Catholic of our days kneel down to the image of the Crucified, quite unheeding whether it be the beautifully finished work of a world-known artist or the badly carved and badly painted puppet from the workshop of some rustic *Hergott-Schnitzer* ; it may be that the devotional fervour with which everything connected with religion was approached by the faithful of the day cast around the illustrative efforts of the school a halo of sanctity which made their absurdities disappear to a sympathising and uncritical onlooker . . . The same conventionalising tendencies as were shown in the treatment of the pure ornament reappear in the drawing and colouring of the human figure . . . In moulding the type of the head the ever-present spiral was resorted to as a capital means of putting the face into the requisite shape, by regulating the troublesome curves of the nose, the mouth and the ears.* This undoubtedly added to the regularity of the type, but unfortunately not to its beauty."

Again, in reference to animal forms, and the conventionalising of them, the same author writes :—

"Here it is, if possible, even more conspicuous. The spiral recurs in the ears, jaws, and junction of the limbs with the body. The whole space of the body is frequently covered with an intricate pattern of some of the ordinary types, and the colours are distributed without the slightest regard to nature."

Again, speaking of Celtic illuminations generally, he says : "And yet they are not so utterly destitute of all artistic merit as some people think. . . . And there are miniature pages, as, for example, in the

---

*A singular example of this artistic coercion will be seen in Plate XVIII., where the top edge of a book is *rounded* so as to be in proper alignment with the nimbus upon which it impinges.

Book of Kells, where the odd formulæ in which the figures appear are in such a singular harmony with the innermost character of the ornaments, and the two elements, miniature and ornament, are so admirably united with a consistent whole of most original aspect, that we are well justified in speaking of a style with reference to similar productions. It might be supposed that a school characterised by the intense Celticism of these and similar productions owed little or nothing to the art of miniature painting as cultivated outside of the Celtic area. Yet this is not the case."

Brunn goes on to show that such paintings are ultimately traceable to non-Celtic models—in other words, to Byzantine or Italo-Byzantine illuminated manuscripts of contemporary or still remoter date. "How this was brought about has yet to be shown."

A much simpler explanation would seem to be that all the *Heraldic* apparently weird figures of either Saviour, saint or man which meet *nature of* us in the pages of the Book of Kells, not to mention other manuscripts *figures.* of about the same period, are, in reality, what might now be termed heraldic. Their being so gives them at once an artistic as well as a theological value. They are heraldic becaues no other form of pictorially personified humanity could be made to fit in with the decorative surroundings in which they are enshrined ; while the deliberate avoidance of any real resemblance to humanity only intensifies the spirit of reverence for holy things possessed by the illuminators. Independently of such reasons, however, it should not be forgotten that the Eastern Church had from an early date laid down very definite instructions in reference to the representation of holy personages ; and undoubtedly such instructions in a pictorial form had reached Ireland from Italy and Southern France at the periods when her school of illumination was in its incipient and its progressive state. These Eastern instructions were long afterwards collected into a book called "The Painter's Guide," which was compiled at Mount Athos, in Greece, from the works of Pauselinos, a painter of the eleventh century, a volume which ultimately became the text-book of Byzantine Art. In a like way the Irish "Book of Ballymote" (A.D. 1300) prescribed the formalities with which the Apostles and other holy personages should be painted ; and there are points in common between the teaching of the two works, as Miss Margaret Stokes has pointed out in her very interesting reference to this subject, though the two manuals

45

are by no means unanimous all through.* For example (amongst many that might be mentioned), in the case of the representation of St. John the Evangelist, the Eastern practice was to paint him as " an old man, bald, large, not very thick beard " ; while the Irish painters were enjoined by both the Book of Ballymote and by the ancient Irish poem in the Codex Maelbrighte to depict him " without any beard."†

Celtic departures from the formalities prescribed by Eastern authority—and they are frequent—would seem to point to the existence of an early traditional treatment of such matters in Ireland which had been followed for perhaps some centuries before the appearance of the Byzantine " Painter's Guide." It is certainly easier to think that the portrait figures of the Book of Kells and similar Irish manuscripts were the direct result of some such local tradition than to assume that the gifted illuminators of the marvellously-drawn decorative portions of such works were unable to paint the human form, had they wished to do so, in a more natural way than they have done.

The smaller illuminations. The smaller illuminated initials, which, owing to their great profusion, would distinguish the Book of Kells from every other manuscript ever written, are reproduced here in a goodly number. Some idea of the total number of these very exquisite gems may be gathered from the fact that, excluding the large illuminations, every verse of every chapter in the four Gospels commences with one of them. Their infinite variety shows an artistic originality of a perfectly bewildering nature. Their beauty of form and colour is reproduced with a rare fidelity in our illustrations (Plates XX to XXIV) which are taken from the copies made by the late Mrs. Helen Campbell D'Olier, of Dublin, a highly-gifted illuminator who devoted a great portion of her life to the work. There are no two of these letters the same throughout the whole volume ; and even the compound letters of the word ET which occur so very many times, never appear twice in the same form. Many of the originals are exhibited in the Library of Trinity College, Dublin.

* " Early Christian Art in Ireland."
† It is worthy of notice that St. John in the Kells Manuscript has fair hair *and* a beard, while the St. John of the Book of Lindisfarne has no beard. The latter deviation is the more remarkable as the Lindisfarne portraits are generally assumed to be more Byzantine than those in the Book of Kells.

The subject of the actual pigments used in the general decoration *The pigments* of the Book of Kells is one of considerable interest ; but it is only from *used in the* comparatively recent investigations that any information has been *MS.* acquired in connection with this obscure branch of Irish palæography. There is as yet no absolute certainty as to either the colours used, or the wonderful durability attaching to them, but microscopic examination has succeeded in rescuing some at least of the materials from oblivion. Professor Hartley, who has gone into the matter more thoroughly than others, gives his conclusions in a paper published in the Proceedings of the Royal Dublin Society, N.S., Vol. IV., 1885 : " A very careful examination of the work shows that the pigments mixed with gum, glue, or gelatine are laid on somewhat thickly—there is no staining of the vellum and no mingling of tints. There is, however, as was pointed out to me, a painting of blue over a ground of green."

His conclusions as to the materials of which the colours are compounded are briefly as follows : The black is lamp black, or possibly fish-bone black ; the bright red is realgar (arsenic disulphide, As_2S_2) ; the yellow, orpiment (arsenic tersulphide, As_2S_3) ; the emerald green, malachite ; the deep blue, possibly lapis-lazuli, but owing to its transparency when overlying green, more likely not so. The reddish-purple is, he thinks, either a finely ground glass coloured with gold, or a preparation like " the purple of Cassius," which is obtained from a solution of gold by the action of a solution of tin, and was extremely costly. It is used very sparingly in the Kells Manuscript, a fact that confirms his view. The other colours used are neutral green, a tint resembling burnt sienna, a pale blue and lilac. Professor Hartley concludes his paper thus :—

" The master who taught the art of designing and painting to the artist who executed the Book of Kells unquestionably knew how to prepare the colours. As for the materials, malachite . . . green in colour, is found near Cork and Limerick ; chrysocolla . . . green to blue in colour, is found in the County Cork ; chrome, hæmatite, and ochres occur in the County Wicklow ; of red hæmatite of an earthy nature, such as is termed raddle, there is a plentiful supply in the County Antrim. Orpiment and realgar must have been obtained from elsewhere, and the purples were undoubtedly of artificial origin ; it is probable they were brought from abroad, and such colours were no doubt treasured as jewels."

47

It remains for me to express my regret at the loss which Trinity College, Dublin, has suffered by the death in 1913 of its late librarian, the Rev. Dr. Abbott, whose scholarly collation of the Book of Kells and other early Irish texts is well known to all students of biblical history. My best thanks are due to Mr. Alfred de Burgh, the sub-librarian, for his courteous assistance and valuable suggestions during my study of the Manuscript.

EDWARD SULLIVAN.

LIST OF PLATES

PLATE I.

A PAGE OF THE EUSEBIAN CANONS.   FOL. 5 R.
(See Introduction, page 7.)

PLATE II.

THE VIRGIN AND CHILD. FOL. 7 V.
(See Introduction, page 8.)

PLATE III.

PORTION OF THE "ARGUMENT" TO THE GOSPEL OF ST. JOHN. FOL. 19 V.

(See Introduction, pages 7 and 9.)

exponitur uescendi desiderio collocato &

quaerentibus fructus laboris & do magiste

rii doctrina seructin

rice sacerdoti appa

ruit angelus & adnuntiauit ei filium ioha

nen & dem mariae adnuntiauit angelus

filium ihm toribus & uca

Natiuitatem ihu adnuntiat angelus pas

pit simeon puerum ihm & benedixit

oin & anna professa bat

& anorum duodecim ihs in templo doce

seniores usmum poenitez

Vbi iohannis baptizat populum bap

PLATE IV.

THE EVANGELICAL SYMBOLS. FOL. 27 V.
(See Introduction, pages 1 o *and* 1 9.)

PLATE V.

PORTRAIT OF ST. MATTHEW. FOL. 28 V.
(See Introduction, pages 11, 13 *and* 14.)

PLATE VI.

THE OPENING WORDS OF ST. MATTHEW'S GOSPEL.
FOL. 29 R.
LIBER
GENE
RATI
ONIS

(*See Introduction, pages* 11. 12, 19 *and* 22.)

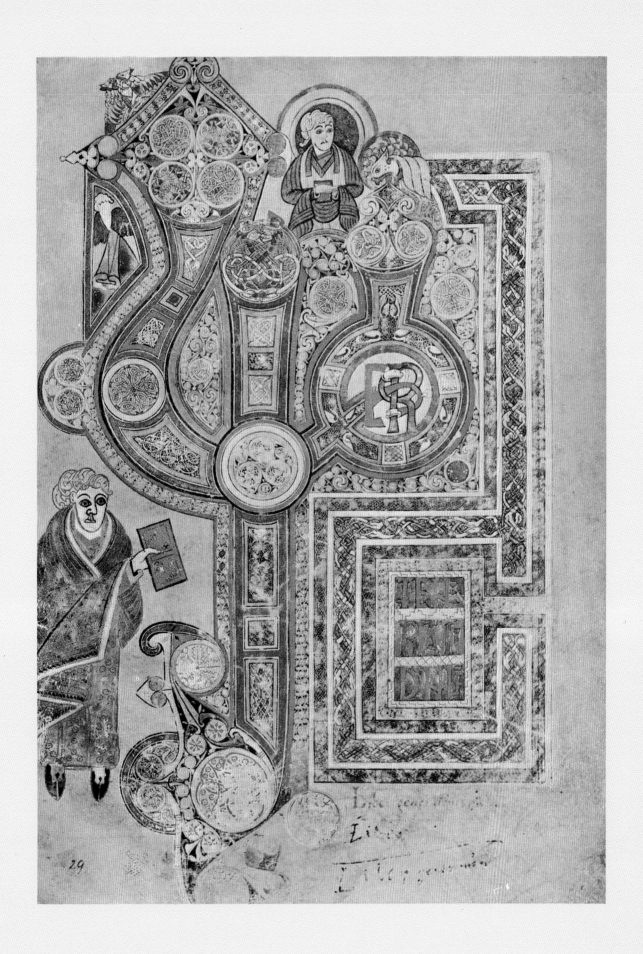

PLATE VII.

PORTRAIT OF ST. MARK OR ST. LUKE. FOL, 32 V,

(See Introduction, pages 1 2, 1 3 *and* 1 4.)

PLATE VIII.

THE EIGHT-CIRCLED CROSS. FOL. 33 R.

(See Introduction, page 15.)

PLATE IX.

THE MONOGRAM PAGE. FOL. 34 R,
XPI B GENERATIO
(Christi autem generatio)
St. Matthew i. 18.
(*See Introduction, pages* 15 *and* 18.)

bgeneraao

PLATE X.

A PAGE OF THE TEXT. FOL. 104 R.
St. Mark. xiii. 17-22.
(*See Introduction, pages 7 and 17.*)

Ae autem pregnantabus et
nutrientabus inillis diebus
Orate autem ut non fiat fuga
uestra hieme uel sabbato
Erit enim tunc tribulatio magna
qualis non fuit abinitio mun
di usque modo neque fiet
Et nisi breuiata fuissent dies
illi non fieret salua om
nis caro sed propter electos bre
uiabuntur dies illi
Tunc siquis uobis dixerit ecce
hic xps aut illic nolite credere
Surgent enim pseudoxpi et
pseudo profetae et dabunt
signa magna et prodigia ita in erro
rem inducantur si fieri potest etiam

PLATE XI.

TUNC CRU
CIFIXERANT
XPI CUM EO DU
OS LATRONES   FOL. 124 R.

St. Matthew xxvii. 38.

(*See Introduction, pages* 18 *and* 19.)

PLATE XII.

THE EVANGELICAL SYMBOLS. FOL. 129 V.
(See Introduction, pages 18 *and* 19.)

PLATE XIII.

THE OPENING WORDS OF ST. MARK'S GOSPEL.
FOL. 130 R
INI TI UM
EVAN GE
LII IHU
XPI

(*See Introduction, pages 18 and 19.*)

PLATE XIV.

THE OPENING WORD OF ST. LUKE'S GOSPEL.
FOL. 188 R.
QUON
IAM

(*See Introduction, page* 19.)

PLATE XV.

THE GENEALOGY OF CHRIST.   FOL. 200 R.

St. Luke iii. 22-26.

FACTA EST TU ES FILIUS MEUS DILECTUS IN TE BENE CONPLACUIT MIHI.
ET IPSE IHS ERAT INCIPIENS QUASI ANNORUM TRIGINTA UT PUTABATUR
FILIUS IOSEPH.

QUI FUIT HELI.

QUI FUIT MATHA.

QUI FUIT LEVI.

QUI FUIT MELCHI.

QUI FUIT IANNAE.

QUI FUIT IOSEPH.

QUI FUIT MATHATHIE.

QUI FUIT AMOS.

QUI FUIT NAUUM.

QUI FUIT ESLI.

QUI FUIT NAGGE.

QUI FUIT MAATH.

(See Introduction, page 20.)

factumest tues filius meus dilectus inte-
bene conplacuit mihi ☩ ❀ ❀ ❀ ❀ ❀ ❀

Ipse ihserat incipiens quasi annorum triginta utputabatur filius

ioseph ❀ ❀ ❀ ❀ ❀

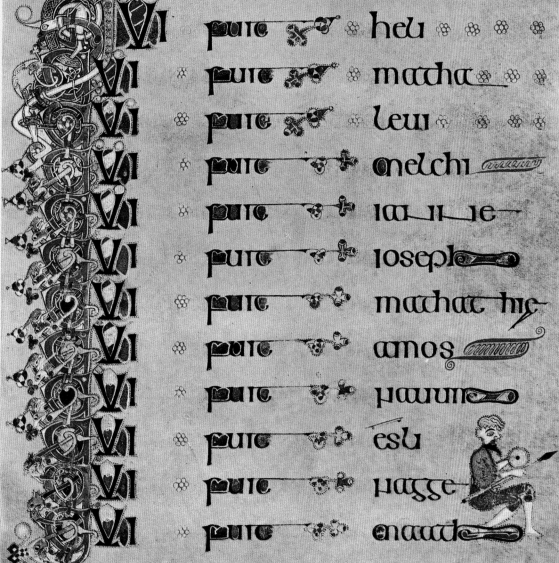

qui fuit heli ❀ ❀ ❀
qui fuit matha ❀ ❀ ❀
qui fuit leui ❀ ❀ ❀
qui fuit melchi
qui fuit iamne
qui fuit ioseph
qui fuit mathat hie
qui fuit amos
qui fuit naum
qui fuit esli
qui fuit nagge
qui fuit maath

PLATE XVI.

THE GENEALOGY—*continued*. FOL. 200 V.

QUI FUIT MATHATH.

QUI FUIT IAE.

QUI FUIT SYMEI.

QUI FUIT IOSEPH. OSSE.

QUI FUIT IUDA.

QUI FUIT JOHANNA.

QUI FUIT RESSAE.

QUI FUIT ZORBBA.

QUI FUIT SALATHIEL.

QUI FUIT NERI.

QUI FUIT MELCHI.

QUI FUIT ADDI.

QUI FUIT COSAM.

QUI FUIT ELMADAM.

QUI FUIT ER.

QUI FUIT IESU.

QUI FUIT ELIEZER.

NOTE.—The two first lines are an uncorrected error. They should read : "QUI FUIT MATHATHIAE" omitting the second "QUI FUIT."

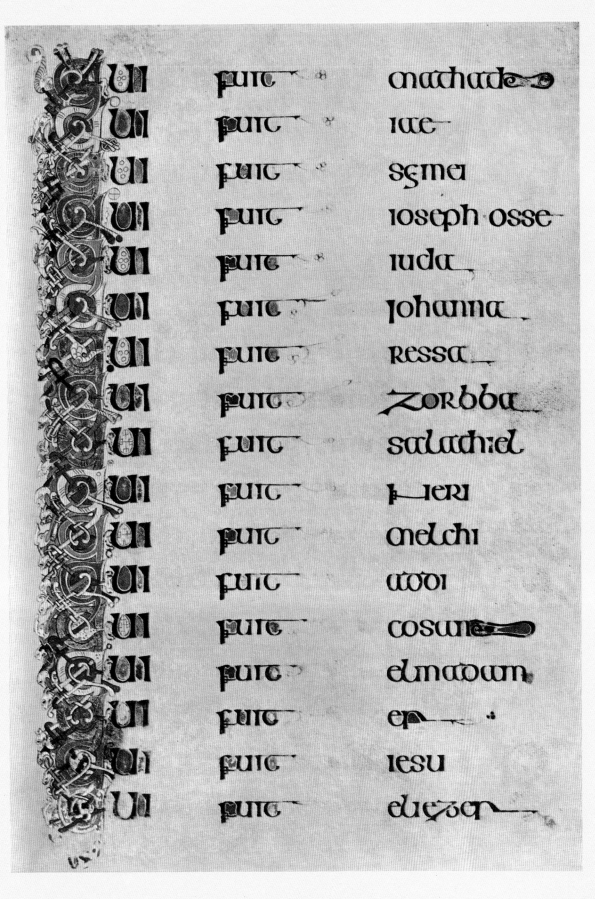

ui	fuit	mecchat
ui	fuit	iae
ui	fuit	semei
ui	fuit	ioseph osse
ui	fuit	iuda
ui	fuit	iohanna
ui	fuit	ressa
ui	fuit	zorbba
ui	fuit	salathiel
ui	fuit	hieri
ui	fuit	melchi
ui	fuit	addi
ui	fuit	cosun
ui	fuit	elmadam
ui	fuit	er
ui	fuit	iesu
ui	fuit	eliezer

PLATE XVII.

THE GENEALOGY—*continued.* FOL. 201 R.

QUI FUIT ZORIM.

QUI FUIT MATHAT.

QUI FUIT LEVI.

QUI FUIT SEMEON.

QUI FUIT IUDA.

QUI FUIT JOSEPH.

QUI FUIT IONA.

QUI FUIT ELIACIM.

QUI FUIT MELCHA.

QUI FUIT MENNA.

QUI FUIT MATHATHIA.

QUI FUIT NATHAN.

QUI FUIT DAVID.

QUI FUIT IESSE.

QUI FUIT OBED.

QUI FUIT BOOS.

QUI FUIT SALMON.

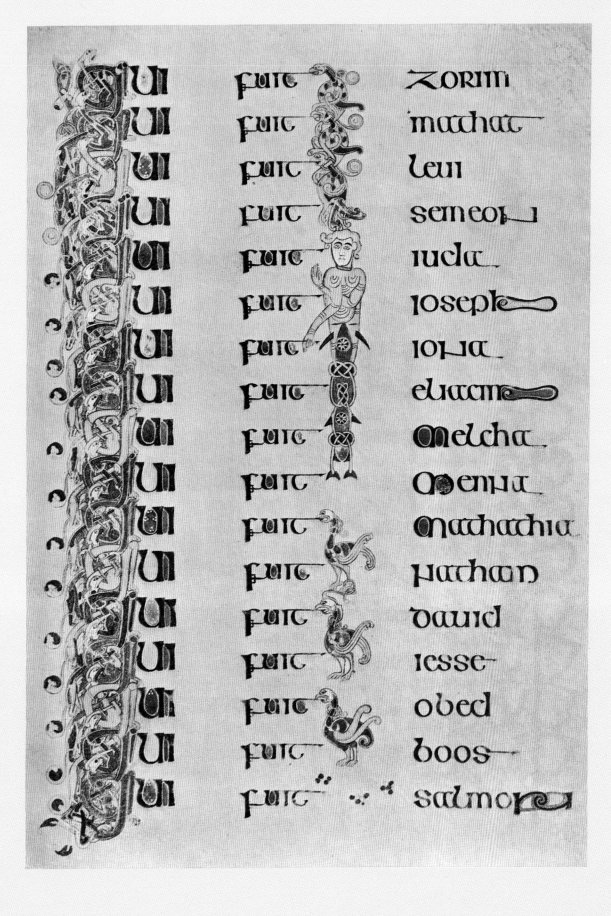

fuit	zorim
fuit	mathat
fuit	leui
fuit	semeon
fuit	iuda
fuit	ioseph
fuit	iona
fuit	eliacim
fuit	melcha
fuit	menna
fuit	mathathia
fuit	nathan
fuit	dauid
fuit	iesse
fuit	obed
fuit	boos
fuit	salmon

PLATE XVIII.

PORTRAIT OF ST. JOHN. FOL. 291 V.

(See Introduction, pages 13, 21 *and* 34.)

NOTE.—This is one of the pages which have suffered most at the hands of the binder, about one hundred years ago. (See Prefatory Note to this volume.)

PLATE XIX.

THE OPENING WORDS OF ST. JOHN'S GOSPEL.
FOL. 292 R.

" In principio erat Verbum et Verbum "—in the following arrangement :

IN   P

RINCI

PIOERAT   VER

     BUMETVERBUM

(*See Introduction, pages* 19 *and* 22.)

PLATE XX.

COMPOUND LETTERS.
(From copies by Helen Campbell D'Olier.)

Q   R   Q

ET

Ad[tendite]   AI
                               AT i[lli]

AD

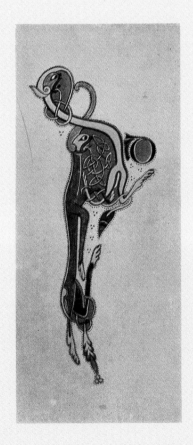

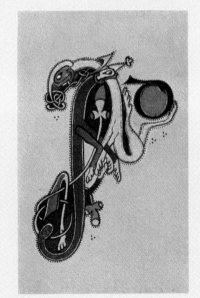

PLATE XXI.

COMPOUND LETTERS.
(From copies by Helen Campbell D'Olier.)

AV   ET DIXit   PO[nite]

Pa[ter]   ID   B[eati]
A[pparuit]   AS   B ,,
                              B ,,
                              B ,,
                              B ,,

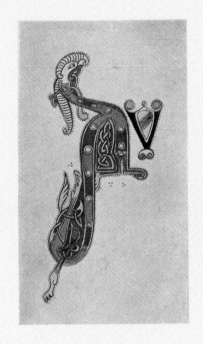

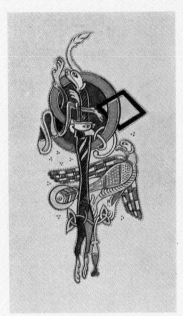

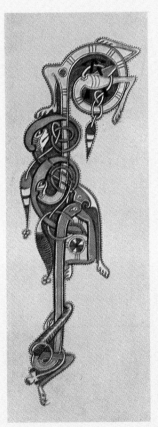
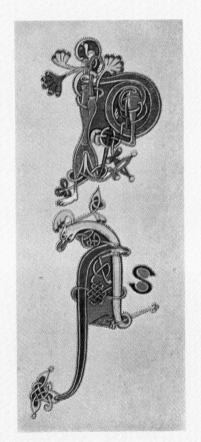

PLATE XXII.

COMPOUND LETTERS.

(From copies by Helen Campbell D'Olier.)

Vesper

Cum ergo

Bonum

Haec

Illis

Ecce

DIco

S

TRadat

PLATE XXIII.

COMPOUND LETTERS.

(From copies by Helen Campbell D'Olier.)

QUi dixit

GEneratio

DIXerunt

SEd neque

PLATE XXIV.

COMPOUND LETTERS.

(From copies by Helen Campbell D'Olier.)

HIc est panis

PRopter

CAvete

EXsurgent

AN ENQUIRY INTO THE ART OF THE ILLUMINATED MANUSCRIPTS OF THE MIDDLE AGES
BY
JOHAN ADOLF BRUUN

CELTIC
ILLUMINATED
MANUSCRIPTS

§ I

N unusually detailed account of a specimen of ancient Celtic art of illumination is contained in a work written by Giraldus Cambrensis and dating from the close of the twelfth century. This author, in his *Topographia Hibernica*, tells us of a marvellous book which came under his notice in the course of his travels in Ireland in the years 1185 and 1186, and commanded his admiration on account of the wonderfully rich and elaborate character of its ornament. The ancient relic, to which he has devoted two chapters in the work containing the *impressions de voyage* of his Irish mission, and which he describes as one of the marvels of Erin, was at that time preserved among the hereditary treasures of the religious foundation of St. Brigid at Kildare. It was a copy of the Four Gospels, traditionally assigned to the days of the patron saint of that house. In its decorative aspect, being deemed too delicate a work for rough human hands, and, besides, too intricate and mysterious an affair for human invention, the book, in accordance with the pious belief of the day, was looked upon by the inmates of the house as a work produced

A

through the kindly assistance of supernatural powers. What arrested the attention of the twelfth century writer, and made him pay such a rare tribute to an object of that kind was not, however, as might be expected, the pious legend of its supernatural origin or high antiquity, but, in the first place, something that fell within the reach of his own personal observation: the manuscript itself, so far as its artistic work was concerned. And the combination of skill, taste, and devoted patience displayed in its ornamental pages is done justice to in the following passage which we extract entire:

»*De libro miraculose conscripto*. Inter universa Kildariæ miracula, nihil mihi miraculosius occurrit quam liber ille mirandus, tempore virginis, ut aiunt, angelo dictante conscriptus. Continet hic liber quatuor Evangeliorum juxta Ieronimum concordantiam: ubi quot paginæ fere tot figuræ diversæ, variisque coloribus distinctissimæ.

Hic Majestatis vultum videas divinitus impressum; hinc mysticas Evangelistarum formas, nunc senas, nunc quaternas, nunc binas alas habentes; hinc aquilam, inde vitulum, hinc hominis faciem, inde leonis; aliasque figuras fere infinitas. Quas si superficialiter et usuali more minus acute conspexeris, litura potius videbitur quam ligatura; nec ullam prorsus attendes subtilitatem, ubi nihil tamen præter subtilitatem. Sin autem ad perspicacius intuendum oculorum aciem invitaveris, et longe penitius ad artis arcana transpenetraveris, tam delicatas et subtiles, tam arctas et artitas, tam nodosas et vinculatim colligatas, tamque recentibus adhuc coloribus illustratas notare poteris intricaturas, ut vere hæc omnia potius angelica quam humana diligentia iam asseveraveris esse composita.

Hæc equidem quanto frequentius et diligentius intueor, semper quasi novis obstupeo, semper magis ac magis admiranda conspicio.«

As to the manner in which the work was composed we are told in the next chapter:

»*De libri compositione*. Nocte prima, cujus mane librum scriptor inchoaturus fuerat, astitit ei angelus in somnis, figuram quandam tabulæ quam manu præferebat impressam ei ostendens, et dicens, »Putasne hanc figuram in prima libri quem scripturus es pagina possis imprimere?» Cui scriptor, de tantæ subtilitatis arte, de tam ignotæ et inusitatæ rei diffidens notitia, respondit, »Nequaquam». Cui angelus, »In crastino die dic dominæ tuæ, ut ispa pro te orationes fundat ad Dominum, quatinus ad acutius intuendum et subtilius intelligendum tibi tam mentis quam corporis oculos aperiat, et ad recte protrahendum manus dirigat.» Quo facto, nocte sequente iterum affuit angelus, eandem figuram aliasque multas ei præsentans. Quas omnes, divina opitulante gratia, statim advertens et memoriæ fideliter commendans libro suo locis competentibus ad unguem scriptor impressit. Sic igitur angelo præsentante, Brigida orante, scriptore imitante, liber est ille conscriptus.» [1]

The latter part of the extract needs no comment. As to the former part of it, containing the personal observations of Giraldus, it should be remembered that such is the opinion of one whom we know, from many traits in his various works, as a shrewd and exact observer, and who, moreover, lived at an epoch when material for comparison, and that of a very high degree of excellence, existed in abundance. In the course of the twelfth century we witness, outside of the Celtic area, a remarkable growth of the art of book-illumination, characterised by volumes of exceptionally grand dimensions and of the most gorgeous decoration in gold and colours. This class of illuminated books seems to have grown into vogue in England in the earlier part of the century, as it did some time previously in the neighbouring countries across the Channel; and there can be little doubt that the zealous and talented Archdeacon of St. David's, who in his earlier years had studied on the Continent, and who became later on so closely allied to the Royal Court of England, was familiar with the literary and artistic aspirations of his own days, and knew to perfection the master-achievements of the non-Celtic schools of art of contemporary date.

Although referring to a particular work of especial merit, the testimony of the mediæval writer may well be placed at the head of an enquiry into the art in general

[1] Giraldi Cambrensis *Opera*, vol. V, pp. 123, 124, London, 1867; in *Rer. Brit. m. æ. script.*

of the Celtic illuminated manuscripts, emphasising as it does at the same time the salient characteristics of the style followed by this distinguished school of illumination: its minute and delicate drawing, its brilliance of colouring, and, above all, that amazing amount of devoted and patient labour which underlies its intricate compositions, and creates the despair of anyone who tries to copy them.

It is proposed in the following pages to give an analysis of the Celtic style of book-decoration, by classifying the various motives or elements of which the complex schemes of an ornamental page are composed; and by tracing the evolution of each separate motive as far as that can be followed in Celtic art; afterwards to deal with the principles of composition and the treatment and effect of colour; and, lastly, to place before the reader a series of works in chronological sequence representative of the school in its successive stages of progress. The question of the historical connexion of Celtic design with that of other countries will be properly treated only after a survey of the other mediæval schools of illumination. Although at first sight presenting a bewildering variety of forms, the designs shown in the decorated manuscripts will, when more closely examined, be seen to submit to a rational classification under four divisions which practically absorb the whole stock of ornament. First, there is a group of patterns in the structure of which purely geometrical combinations or developments of the straight or curved line form the sole element. Then, we have groups of motives which, though anything but natural, yet were originally derived from Nature, such as highly conventionalised schemes of animals, leaves, and flowers. And, finally, there is a group of figure subjects or representations suggested by the accompanying text, which, owing to an emphatically decorative treatment, may be looked upon as mere decoration rather than illustration. Accordingly, the four divisions will be: — (1) geometrical ornament; (2) zoomorphic and (3) phyllomorphic designs; and (4) figure representations.

II

ELTIC ornament as shown in the pages of the illuminated manuscripts receives its most characteristic and most national element from the group of *spiral* designs. The spiral is a motive of high antiquity in Celtic decorative art. From a number of objects dating from a period anterior to the introduction of Christianity into Ireland, it appears that a peculiar type of spiral was a staple design to the pagan Celt; and if we compare the spiral patterns of pagan origin with those exhibited in the various works of Christian art in Ireland, the illuminated manuscripts included, there can be little doubt that the spiral system of the Christian centuries was lineally descended from that known in earlier times to the pagan natives of the country. We hope to prove this suggestion to be something more than a vague hypothesis. The spiral design was no accidental feature in the pagan Celtic art; nor was it confined to such simple, uniform scrolls as those we find used as a kind of border ornament by several pre-historic peoples. It was, on the contrary, a favourite pattern of a very elaborate character, applied as a surface decoration to a variety of objects, such as shields, helmets, sword-sheaths, armlets, horse-trappings, and personal ornaments, examples of which still survive, testifying to an astonishing proficiency in metal work — bronze and gold — both as regards construction and decoration.[1] The ornament that lends the higher dignity to these and similar objects — the pride of the Celtic warrior and chieftain — consists of a most characteristic spiral design which, though simple and abstract, yet at the same time possesses a peculiar

[1] The most representative collections of objects decorated with the late Celtic spiral work found in the British Islands, are in the British Museum; and in the National Museum of Ireland [R. I. A. coll.] in Dublin. For illustrations, the reader should refer to *Archæologia*, vol. XXXVI, plate XXXVII; vol. XL, plates XXX, XXXI; vol. LIV, plate XLVIII; vol. XLVII, plate XXI; to the publications of the R. I. A., for ex., *Transactions R. I. A.*, vol. XXX, part V, plate XIX, with beautiful reproduction in colours; and to plates in Kemble's *Horæ Ferales*, also in colours. For lists of objects, see the descriptions added by Sir A. Wollaston Franks in Kemble's *op. cit.* p. 125 *seqq.*; and also later volumes of *Archæologia*.

force combined with a flamboyant elegance in its long, sweeping curves. This is the style of ornament to which Sir Augustus Wollaston Franks has given the name of *late Celtic*. The root from which it sprang is uncertain. It has been suggested that, at least in some types, it was developed under the influence of floral or foliated schemes transplanted from classical ground.[1] If so, that might account for part of its force and freedom, qualities so rare in an ornament of purely geometrical extraction; while, on the other hand, in case the opinion be correct, the Celtic pattern may be said to be the most ingenious translation ever made, of a foliageous design into a geometrical one. Here, as in every spiral system, the principal elements are a series of volutes and the links which connect them together. But what lends to this a character of its own is the special development of the connecting links which, by gradually expanding or contracting, enrich the ornament with a series of long, slender curves of great linear beauty. The pattern usually appears in relief produced either by *repoussé* work and chasing, when the object was made of plates of metal wrought into shape with the hammer and rivetted together; or by the particular form given to the mould, in the case of casting. On works of the first description the links bounded by the long curved lines are raised above the surface so as to present a section with a sharp ridge at the top. The artistic appearance effected by the bold design and energetic modelling of the late Celtic spiral ornament is further enhanced by the application of *champ-levé* enamel[2], used on plaques or bosses attached to the pattern to emphasise the centres of the volutes, etc. Objects exhibiting this style of decoration have been discovered in various districts of Great Britain and Ireland, showing the style to have been at one time common to

[1] See especially *Archæologia*, vol. LII, p. 317 *seqq.*, 364 *seqq.*, in which Mr. Arthur Evans contributes some very important notes on the connexions between late Celtic forms of ornament and classical art in its archaic as well as later stages.
[2] See especially coloured plates with descriptions in Kemble's *op. cit.*; *Transactions R. I. A.*, vol. XXX, part. V, pp. 277, 281, with coloured plate XIX; *cfr. Archæologia*, vol. XLVI, pp. 83, 84, 89.

the pre-Christian Celtic population of the British Islands. Besides, similar objects have been found, although more sparsely, on the tracks of Celtic tribes on the Continent, whereas, outside of regions known to have been, in a bygone age, inhabited or visited by such tribes, there is little analogous to it, and nothing of an altogether similar nature. This seems to prove the so-called late Celtic, whatever may be its germ or its prototype, to have claim to be regarded as an emphatically Celtic style of art. And as such it flourished at the time when the Christian missionaries carried to the pagan Celts the faith and rites of a new religion together with the principles of a new art.

What was the actual result effected at this meeting of foreign and native elements: how they tend to modify each other, and both of them influence the following evolution, will be shewn by a most instructive parallel afforded by the history of architecture. A series of ecclesiastical buildings, some of which are found surrounded by the dry-built cells within the boundary walls of the ancient monastic communities, while others are situated in isolated positions without any connexion with other structures, enable us to trace the evolution of the typical forms of the Celtic church in Ireland, from the earliest centuries of Irish Christianity until, in the course of the twelfth century, it appears as a special, well-defined variety of the Romanesque style of architecture. The late Lord Dunraven, in his great work on Irish architecture, has made these venerable remnants, extending through a period the architectural history of which is almost a blank in the other countries of Europe north of the Alps, a subject for most careful research. He has pointed out how the most primitive of these churches belong to a type which still bears the impress of the transitional stage between paganism and Christianity.[1] Thus, while the principles and methods of construction are the very same as those

[1] *Notes on Irish Architecture,* by Edwin, third Earl of Dunraven; edited by Margaret Stokes; vol. I, London, 1875; p. 26 *seqq.*; vol. II, London, 1877; p. 134 *seqq.*

shown in works of purely pagan origin, a special plan and arrangement of the room, differing from what may be observed in any pagan structure, clearly indicates their ecclesiastical purpose. He also lays stress upon the fact that the following evolution nowhere shows any sudden break in the continuity of style, but only a gradual advance towards those more elaborate types which prevailed in countries nearer the centres of Christian civilization.[1] And in following his guidance we observe how constructive peculiarities of the greatest importance, as, for example, the ingenious practice of the Irish »double stone roof»,[2] were, after all, but the results that gradually and rationally, under the influence of the foreign elements, grew out of the primitive devices of the pagan natives.

The reader will excuse this little digression, running off on a somewhat diverging line from our spirals. It has been done in order to show that, if we should find in the evolution of decorative art, when passing the point marked by the change of religion, an analogon to the state of things observable in the sphere of architecture, that is precisely what might be expected.

The spiral decoration as shown in the pages of the illuminated manuscripts may be briefly defined as a system of volutes closely coiled in circular curves, and connected each with a varying number of adjoining volutes. In its most typical form it appears as a chain composed of links almost invariably C-shaped, hooking together. This chain is carried over the space to be decorated so as to cover it with its coils as closely as possible. The space, however, often being very irregular, some difficulty was experienced in thus filling in all nooks and corners; and an expedient was found either in making volutes of different size so as to fit or in introducing additional links into the chain. By this method the triple and quadruple spirals arose, while at the same time the intricacy, not only of the convolutions, but of the whole design was greatly

[1] *Op. cit.,* vol. II, pp. 200, 202.
[2] *Op. cit.,* vol. II, p. 196.

increased. These complex patterns were further developed by an ingenious arrangement combining volutes of different size in symmetrical compositions to fill in, for instance, a circular space. This is a favourite device in the manuscripts of the best period, and one which shows the spiral pattern in its most perfect elaboration. In the decadent age of Celtic book-decoration the spiral ornament disappears earlier than any of the other designs.

If we compare the so-called late Celtic spiral decoration with that of the illuminated manuscripts, we find at a glance, in spite of an unmistakable resemblance, some marked features of difference. These latter, however, may all be easily accounted for. An ornamental design when transplanted from one object to another of different material is necessarily submitted to some modifications due to material, technique, size and shape of the surface, etc.; and so was of course the ornament in question when transferred from a bold metal surface to the diminutive space afforded by the initial or border compartment of an illuminated folio. There it extended freely with long, mighty curves and slender volutes over a field more than sufficient; here the space was so limited as to admit of but the smallest possible vacancies; hence, the reduced curves of the links and the more intricate character of the convolutions, which the pen of the illuminator was better fitted than the instrument of the metal-worker to run in a number of turns round the centre. The link joining a couple of volutes on the late Celtic bronzes is often bent into the curve of the letter S, whereas in the spiral system of the illuminated manuscripts the connecting link is seen to follow almost invariably the curve of a C. What led to a more general adoption of the latter form was, no doubt, its being a means of joining the volutes so as to cover as closely as possible a surface even of less regular shape.

There are, however, apart from the general scheme of the ornament, some details which deserve a special notice, as testifying in a most significant way to the actual connexion between the late Celtic system and that

B

108

of the Christian period. Such details may be seen in the decorative treatment of the centres of the volutes as well as of the central portions of the links. The centre of a volute designed on the minute scale typical of Celtic book-ornamentation does not seem to be a suitable place for the insertion of additional adornment; and yet, strange to say, we generally find this point emphasised by a variety of additional devices. Very often these take the shape of a circular space worked with a diminutive pattern which consists of some kind of chequered or diapered design; or of the ends of the coils wound up into secondary spirals or expanding into heads or even full forms of birds and nondescripts in symmetrical arrangement. On the link we observe a curious little thing in the shape of an almond placed across its central portion, from the point where the two front curves meet in a cusp, towards the middle of the back curve. This little figure is seen repeated in a similar position to relieve the triangular empty spaces intervening between the curved boundaries of links and volutes. In the complex patterns of triple and quadruple spirals this gives rise to what might seem at first sight to be a foliageous scheme. The little trefoil thus produced has, however, nothing to do with the department of botany. It owes its origin simply to an accidental repetition of the single oval stamped in the middle of the link. And this in its turn is a reminiscence of the oval boss which we have noticed in a similar position on the late Celtic metal work; just as the ornamented circular plaques of enamel attached to the centres of the volutes on pagan bronzes may have suggested the circular spaces with varied decoration which mark the starting point of the convolution in the spiral system of the Christian period. A reminiscence of the pattern from which that of the manuscripts was originally derived once being raised in relief, is still to be observed in the latter. The small triangular spaces intervening between the curved outlines of links and volutes, and corresponding to the background of the late Celtic pattern, are, as a rule, marked by a darker colour and thus characterised as having once formed a recessed background.

Although most common and best developed in the complex patterns which are employed to fill in, as a surface decoration, the small sections into which the space of the initial or border is divided, the spiral very often appears as a plain scroll forming an ornamental appendix to the extremities of the initial. And in a few cases it will be seen to have influenced the initial also in its structural aspect. Examples of this type, in which the little oval of late Celtic extraction is still discernible, may be seen in the ancient Irish Psalter traditionally assigned to the time of St. Columba and now preserved in the library of the Royal Irish Academy.[1]

In the previous pages the spiral system as applied to the decoration of illuminated manuscripts has been delineated in its general scheme; its characteristics and development followed in some detail; and its relation to the style of art exhibited in late Celtic metal work briefly considered. What has been said may prove enough to show that this type of pattern, one of the chief elements of Christian decorative art in Ireland, and of especial significance as a testimony to the minute elaboration and marvellous finish of detail characteristic of the Celtic school of illumination, is the survival of an earlier native system, which, although submitted to various modifications in being applied to quite new purposes, yet has left, along the whole line of derived forms, an impress sufficiently clear and well-defined for its origin to be easily recognised. Some might claim the spiral design of Christian art in Ireland as having originated independently. We do not intend to enter into a discussion of that as it is but an hypothesis, supported neither by historical evidence nor by analogies. On the other hand, one might think of its being introduced together with the stock of ornament brought from other countries by the early Christian missionaries. But it would be very difficult, if not impossible, to point to a single scheme in de-

[1] The *Cathach MS.*, Libr. R. I. A., Dublin.

corative art outside of the Celtic area with greater claim
than the so-called late Celtic to be considered as the prototype that once suggested the spiral design shown in
manuscripts and other works of the Christian era.

THE next room after the spiral ornament we
may place an important group consisting of geometrical *interlacements*. This type of pattern as
appearing in the illuminated manuscripts may be
characterised as a surface decoration composed
of one or more ribbons or straps of uniform size,
which are twisted, plaited, knotted, or otherwise
interwoven so as to cover the field with a symmetrically disposed design. It occurs in a variety of
forms, from the plain twist, or guilloche, to the elaborate
chain composed of knots of torturing intricacy and of
varied construction, being laid in squares, circles, oblongs, triangles, hexagons, octagons, etc. The more
intricate forms are predominant; and, by variety of design and the unerring precision with which the ribbons
are interwoven so as to cross over and under alternately and finally be joined up to each other, testify
to the astonishing capacity of the draughtsman. When
compared with the spiral ornament, the interlaced work
looks rather mechanical. This is particularly the
case with the plainer forms, in which the linear
element is confined to a monotonous repetition of
the same kind of curve. Hence it came that these never
obtained great favour, but held a very subordinate place
to the more complicated patterns. An interlaced series
would receive an additional enrichment in various ways.
One method was to lay it with alternate patches of colour,
producing at the same time the effect of some kind of
chequer work. While some of the more complex patterns
still present in their structure the endless repetition of the
same kind of curve, the linear element of others is developed with a very pleasing result by straight lines being
introduced to serve as a backbone to the ornament; as also
by curves broken into the shape of a section of a pointed

arch being made to alternate with those following an even circular path. Besides, there are forms in which the interlaced work was disposed so as to leave blank spaces alternating with the elaborate knot work. By these and similar means a certain measure of freedom and variety was introduced into the ornament. Designs of the nature just described are seen repeated again and again, with slight variations, in the works of the best period, and may be regarded as typical of Celtic interlaced work as instanced in illuminated manuscripts. Interlacings of an altogether angular character are rarely met with in works of the earlier centuries, as in pages of the *Book of Durrow;*[1] they seem to belong chiefly to forms marking the degradation of style of a later period.

Before leaving the subject of interlacements we must not omit mention of a particular use of these designs in being applied to the construction of initials. Smaller initials heading the sub-divisions of the text will be seen at an early period to be worked on the principle of an intertwining strap work; but the chief development of this type of letter seems to fall within the later era, when the method gives rise to a peculiar character that might be defined as a piece of purely geometrical interlacing, with nondescript beasts' heads occasionally attached to the terminations. This type in its turn was further developed by transforming the geometrical strap work with its zoomorphic ends into a complete scheme of a nondescript animal with head, legs, and tail; or into a composition of similar creatures. And details such as ears, and crests, and tails, were in that case prolonged and extenuated into endless appendices, and twisted and woven at random around the broader structural body. Initial letters of this nature, enriched with patches of colour in the interior spaces, form the chief decorative feature of the illuminated manuscripts of the period when the Celtic style of book-decoration was on the decline. They show a marked contrast to the grand

[1] *MS. A. 4. 5.,* Trinity College, Dublin.

ornamental initials of the culminating art; but although unquestionably inferior with regard to minute drawing and accuracy of detail, yet from a certain boldness of design and broader treatment of colour they receive, not infrequently, an artistic, picturesque stamp. In a somewhat rough execution the type appears in works dating from the last centuries of the Middle Ages; and may almost be said to have survived the mediæval art of book-ornamentation, as it is still to be seen in manuscripts written after the introduction of printed books. Thus the *MS. Life of St. Columba*, by Manus O'Donel, chief of Tir Connell, written in the earlier half of the sixteenth century and now preserved in the library of the Franciscan Convent in Dublin,[1] still presents, at the commencement of the volume, a large initial letter of the type described, drawn in outline and partly laid with colour after the old mediæval fashion.

A third group of geometrical motives of decoration we include the several varieties of *fret* work. Like the spiral and interlaced work, this kind of ornament was employed to fill in small panels as part of the surface enrichment of borders and initials. A rectilinear design, composed of a system of straight strokes, which are symmetrically disposed so as to meet at definite angles, but never overlap, and only rarely flow into a curve, the fret may be easily distinguished from all kinds of interlaced work. On the other hand, in spite of the different aspect, it has several features in common with the spiral design. When more closely examined, the fret, plain or complex, will reveal a series of centres disposed at regular intervals over the space to be decorated. Each of these centres marks the starting point for what forms the groundwork of the design, viz., a small figure in the shape of a ⊏ or an ⊑, corresponding to the C- or S-shaped links in the spiral systems. In fact, every variety of fret, even of the

§ IV

[1] *MS. G VIII,* Libr. Franc. Conv., Dublin.

most hopelessly labyrinthine nature, can be derived from a mechanical combination and repetition of these primary elements. By means of the **⊏**- or **Ƽ**-shaped links each centre is connected with one or more adjoining centres. And the plain or composite character of the ornament chiefly depends on the number of links thus starting from the same centre. In the simplest and best known of fret patterns, the plain Greek *mœander,* we find a continuous chain composed of similar links; and, again, in the most intricate forms of Celtic fret there is nothing but a mechanical composition of the same simple groundwork. What lends to the Celtic fret a character of its own, contrasting with that of the square type so common in Greek art, was the fashion of bending the links at certain points at angles of 45°, instead of 90°, which latter are exclusively used in the square type. Hence they appear in the slightly modified forms of a **ɼ** or a **Ƽ**; and from this procedure the pattern as a whole will receive a peculiar Chinese-looking weaving with lines plying in three directions, a diagonal one being added to the horizontal and vertical paths followed by the line of the square type. This kind of fret, characterised by lines which are drawn diagonally over the space, on being broken at angles of 45° alternating at definite points with right angles, became a standard design owing to the more elaborate structure and greater variety introduced by the diagonal element.

In the illuminated manuscripts the fret appears in a variety of forms, from plain, continuous chains to elaborate compositions of what might be styled the quadruple fret, *i. e.,* four links issuing from the same centre. Here, as was the case with the interlaced work, the more complex forms are prevalent; and regarding the shape of the little figure that forms the groundwork of the design, the patterns are mostly seen to be derived from that broken at angles of 45°. Hence, the predominance of the diagonal types. In fact, the Celtic fret patterns would seem at first sight to be all built on that principle. But such is not the case. For, if we follow the lines of the main design, we

114

shall find them invariably deflecting at right angles and thus
pursuing their path in two directions only, either horizon-
tally or vertically; just as do the lines of the regular square
build. What makes these patterns look diagonal is the
relation of the main design to the enclosing border. In
order to lessen the stiffness and monotony of the ornament by making its lines break with those of the border,
the pattern as a whole was turned a little and placed diagonally on the panel to be decorated, its lines cutting
those of the border at an angle of 45°, instead of being
run parallel. It will be seen, then, that the small triangular spaces which result from the border lines being brought
into contact with those of the pattern, are simply due to
the necessity of adjusting the surface design to the border,
and have nothing to do with the main build of the ornament. There is another point about the Celtic fret which
is at first sight a little puzzling, and makes the structure
of the ornament look a more serious affair than it really
is. This is due to the designer not being always quite
sure as to what was the actual background of his ornament. Let us take a quadruple fret of the square type.
Here we see four links issuing from the same centre, each
joining with its other end a similar centre, much in the
same way as do the four coils of a quadruple spiral. This
is the real groundwork of the design. But, at the same
time, the empty spaces intervening between the links will
be seen to form another pattern of a rectilinear type, which,
although bearing a close resemblance to the actual pattern,
yet is not altogether identic. Now, in the illuminated
manuscripts the ornamental design and its background are
of different colour. In the works of the best period it is
a rule to have the design, of whatever description, brought
out in relief by the application of darker and stronger
tones to the background. The difference between pattern
and background with regard to colouring is also observed
in the case of fret work; but what might here cause some
confusion, and obviously shows that the designer did not
quite grasp the meaning of his ornament, is that, while,

as a rule, the real design is brought out as it should, there are other cases in which the rectilinear spaces which form the background are raised and treated as the actual ornament.

What still remains unnoticed of geometrical decoration is either of less importance or of too rare occurrence to be regarded as characteristic of the style in general. One noteworthy feature is the use of *dots*, in single or repeated rows, to emphasise the outline of the initial. This is observable in the earliest extant manuscripts, as, for example, in the ancient Psalter mentioned above; and continues in fashion to the very end. From the large initial the punctured line would extend to embrace the other more or less decorative letters in the same page; and in the richest works, in which, according to a fashion known in other styles of book-illumination, the letters were laid on decorative bands, this kind of background is seen to be worked with patterns that were, not infrequently, dotted or punctured out on the same principle.

Diaper work will be seen to be occasionally introduced to enliven smaller spaces and vacancies between the broader and more elaborate designs. But this stiffest of all geometrical elements never played any great part in Celtic decoration. Several varieties of it may be seen in the pages of the *Book of Kells*, where it occurs together with *rosettes*, a decidedly non-Celtic detail of ornament.

And with this we may lay aside the chequered variety of geometrical designs, a class of ornament which embraces the main mass of patterns to be found in the illuminated manuscripts.

ET the series of patterns which is next to be §V considered still includes sufficient variety of types of a pronounced Celtic character to form important co-ordinate classes. In these we group the ornamental designs in which a copying of natural forms is more or less conspicuous. It must be distinctly understood, however, that in speaking thus we do not mean to assert that any

C

object was represented naturally. For quite the reverse is the case. In most instances the decorative form is as different as it possibly could be from the forms of any object in actual existence. Among the *zoomorphic* schemes there are birds, quadrupeds of a nondescript nature, sometimes even the utterly contorted outline of a human figure. As to the birds and quadrupeds it would be of no use to be too particular in any attempt to trace their zoological prototypes. Regarding the former the most outstanding features are such as might be derived by decorative treatment from almost any variety of the species; and in the case of the latter the origination is, if possible, still more hopelessly obscured.

An observation connecting these forms with some hybrid figures, half nature, half fancy, which occur in their close vicinity, might perhaps settle the question. If we compare details, such as heads, limbs, and wings, in the zoomorphic interlacings with corresponding details in the representations of the Evangelistic symbols, which are a stock design in the illuminated copies of the Gospels, we find, in the majority of cases, a striking resemblance. This naturally suggests the idea that the ancient symbols, such as the eagle of St. John or the lion of St. Mark, repeated from copy to copy in traditional schemes, once served as the originals from which the designer gathered the zoomorphic details for his fanciful pieces of decoration. Hence we may fairly set aside the speculations on the zoological prototypes as rather unnecessary, the more so, because the peculiar nature of this kind of ornament depends — not so much on details as on the manner in which these are connected together so as to form a consistent whole. A zoomorphic interlacing used, like the forms of ornament we have been dealing with, to fill in a panel or compartment of more or less regular shape will be seen, in most cases, to arise from the repetition of a single figure, a bird or a quadruped, with head, legs, wings of a distinct, well-defined type attached to a curious, decoratively treated piece of a body. According to the shape of the space to be adorned, the figure is repeated to form either a continuous chain or a composite group of two or four specimens in symmetrical arrangement, which group in its turn is capable of repetition. Occasionally we find a composition of two figures of different type, for example, a bird and a quadruped. This group is also capable of further combination and repetition. The chief trait common to all these varieties is the great pains taken in twisting, plaiting, and weaving them together in every conceivable manner. When the tangle produced by intertwining the limbs, tail, neck, and trunk of the body was not deemed sufficient, some further devices had to be invented. One was to prolong the jaw, the crest, or the top of the ear into a sort of appendix intended to serve as an additional link.

The animal element also appears in the terminations of borders and initials. One very favourite method was to add a beast's head and a pair of legs at one end of the border; and if we follow the long, broken band covered with decorative panels, we should not be surprised at finding the rest of the body attached to the other end in the shape of a pair of diminutive hind-legs. Or, there is another border run right round the page, with a human head at the top, a pair of feet at the lower margin, and an arm attached to each side! Occasionally the large ornamental initials are seen to be treated in a similar manner. In specimens of the decadent period it is a rule to use zoomorphic terminals for the interlaced work which does duty for the body of the letter; a type from which evolved that composed of a complete animal figure or of a combination of such, as has been shown above. The peculiarities of the various types will be explained by the accompanying plates better than by words. There we see the form typical of the zoomorphic interlacements in the *Book of Durrow*. It consists of a body in the shape of a curved or undulating band, with fore-leg, hind-leg, a dull, tame head, and elongated jaws. There is, perhaps, along the whole line of animal motives used in decorative art, none more utterly stripped of animal life and expression, in being transformed according to the laws of a certain conventionalising principle. A marked contrast to this type is shown in the pages of the *Book of Kells*[1] and the *Gospels of Lindisfarne.*[2] There we often meet with a head suggestive of a beast of prey, but rather exaggerating the bloodthirsty propensities of its zoological prototype. It mostly occurs at the end of a border or an initial, and may often be seen side by side with the lifeless schemes of the Durrow type. In the zoomorphic interlacements of the decadent period, when they appear chiefly in the structure of initials, the head assumes a variety of forms according to the whims of the draughtsman. Thus in the *Liber Hymnorum*[3] from which the initials in the present work are drawn, and which seems to date from the eleventh century, among the number of beasts' heads worked in the letters there is hardly one quite like another; and yet, at the same time, they have such features in common as testify to their derivation from the types in use at earlier periods. The bird frequently figures in the works of the best period. Its chief characteristics are a long beak curved at the end, a well developed wing, which, like part of the body, is covered with various kinds of feather pattern, and a remarkably well drawn leg. It is seen in profile, as are the animal motives with very few exceptions.

Other animal forms than those now described are of rare or exceptional occurrence. Such is the case with the fish and the serpent, both of which may be seen among the curiosities of the *Book of Kells*. Here they are chiefly used as ornamental finials; the fish also doing duty for the sign of abbreviation in, for example, the monogrammatic contraction *IHS*. Occasionally we find, as in the *Books of Kells* and *Armagh*[4], a letter partly formed of the figure of a fish, according to a fashion well-known in Merovingian and Lombardic manuscripts. In some cases the human

[1] *MS. A. 1. 6.*, Trinity Coll., Dublin.
[2] *Cotton. MS. Nero D. 4.*, Brit. Mus.
[3] *MS. E. 4. 2.*, Trinity Coll., Dublin.
[4] *MS.* (no press-mark) Trinity Coll., Dublin.

figure was made use of for decorative purposes. Thus a human head may be seen attached to the end of a letter or a border; or a group of dreadfully contorted bodies made to fill in a small panel or a circular compartment.

OTIVES derived from other departments of nature, §VI such as leaves, flowers, and fruit of *plants*, never played any great part in Celtic ornament. So far as evidence at present goes, they may be said to have been utterly ignored, if not quite unknown, for a length of time. There are manuscripts, among those most lavishly decorated, in which it would be impossible to detect, even by the most careful examination, the slightest shade of a floral or foliageous design. There is nothing of the kind in the *Book of Durrow*[1]; nor in the *Book of Dimma*[2]; nor in the *Gospels of Mac Durnan* , and in the most beautiful and perfect specimen of Hibernian art as cultivated outside of its native isle, the *Gospels of Lindisfarne,* the plant ornament is likewise conspicuous by its absence. Nor does it seem, when once introduced, ever to have become very fashionable. Together with some other devices obviously due to an influx of foreign ideas it appears in the *Book of Kells,* engrafted, with as good grace as possible, on the national stock of ornament. After this epoch, in spite of its growth in the most brilliant work of Irish caligraphy and book-illumination, it will never well prosper. Occasionally we meet with a small panel filled in with what seems to be intended for a scroll of foliage; but, as a rule, the leaf design only survives in the very subordinate position of an appendix or termination ornament, where, moreover, under a not very careful treatment it loses its character, and dwindles into a semi-geometrical scheme, the true origin of which requires some thought and comparison to be detected.

[1] *MS. A. 4. 5.,* Trinity Coll., Dublin.
[2] *MS. A. 4. 23.,* Trinity Coll., Dublin.
[3] *MSS. collect.,* Archiepiscopal Library, Lambeth.

In the *Book of Kells* there are several varieties, the most typical being that of a scroll which branches out at various points, with a trefoil or a palmetto-shaped leaf of four or five leaflets terminating each of the branches. In the most elaborate scheme two scrolls of this description will be seen to proceed from a vase, and extend each on its side, with leaves and tendrils carefully intertwined so as to cover the space with a symmetrical pattern. Or, in a somewhat plainer shape it appears as a single undulating stem with scrolls in the hollows alternately on the right and left. The phyllomorphic element recurs in combinations with zoomorphic details. Thus a scroll proceeding from between the open jaws of a nondescript beast's head, and a trefoil-shaped leaf attached to the other end of the creature are common devices. In addition to these there are scrolls of foliage with complete animal forms of the types described introduced amongst the branches. A floral or foliated scheme, drawn in outline, frequently figures as a sort of flourish appended to smaller initials or even plain letters in the text; and similar free-hand sketches recur among the bewildering variety of ornamental designs at the beginning or the end of the ordinary line or in the vacant space left between two sentences. The method of working the tail or the tongue of a nondescript into the shape of foliage was obviously deemed a great invention. This is the principal position in which the phyllomorphic element survives in works of later times. We rarely meet with a scroll extending over a panel, as in the *Book of Kells;* but the leaf appendix of the animal body is of so frequent occurrence that it may be regarded as one of the leading characteristics of the designs of the decadent age. Most of the forms of leaf in this position are traceable to those shown in the *Book of Kells,* the trefoil and quatrefoil, as well as the lanceolate and heart-shaped types. An innovation appears with the introduction of the leaf with the tricuspid profile, a type characteristic of Carlovingian art and afterwards a stock design in almost every dialect of Romanesque ornament. Only we should not expect to find anything like a fair copy of the original. The conventionalising principle asserts itself here as elsewhere, regulating the outline. The gracefully curved leaf becomes a stiff and formal affair with a contour drawn on the spiral idea. Near the point where the curved boundaries of the longest leaflet meet, we often observe a little oval figure laid across the leaflet. In its present position it appears quite enigmatic and out of place. What does it mean? And where did it come from? The little figure points back to our starting point, the pre-Christian art of Ireland. It is a hall-mark connecting some of the latest and most debased types of Hibernian ornament as exhibited in the illuminated manuscripts with the ancient native art of the Isle, by testifying to the influence of the spiral principle in moulding and regulating Celtic design down to the very end of its national existence.

LASTLY, we come to the subject of *figures* and § VII *scenes* intended to serve as illustrations for the sacred books. As such they do not lack interest although they are of less value from the point of view of art. For it should be stated at the outset that, whatever were the attainments of the Celtic school of miniature-painters, they were assuredly no masters in the art of figure-drawing. It may be that this very imperfect style of draughtsmanship, which appears to modern onlookers so ridiculously childish and grotesque, was viewed by its contemporaries with a very different eye from that with which a modern critic views the same thing. It may be that the absurdities in form and colour, which make the figures of the Saviour and his Apostles appear to us like so many rudely expressed travesties, were veiled by a sentiment similar to that which makes the pious Catholic of our days kneel down to the image of the Crucified, quite unheeding whether it be the beautifully-finished work of a world-known artist or the badly carved and badly painted puppet from the workshop of some rustic *Herrgott-Schnitzer;* it may be that the devotional fervour with which everything connected with religion was approached by the faithful of the day cast around the illustrative efforts of the school a halo of sanctitude which made their absurdities disappear to a sympathising and uncritical onlooker. But still it may be asked with reference to those who executed the work: How was it possible to combine with the consummate skill displayed in the elaboration of the purely ornamental such an utter inability in figure-drawing as that revealed in the monstrous productions of the Celtic school of miniature-painting?

The same conventionalising tendencies as were shown in the treatment of the pure ornament reappear in the drawing and colouring of the human figure. Of actual observation and imitation of nature there is very little, indeed. In moulding the type of the head the ever-present spiral was resorted to as a capital means of putting the face into the requisite shape, by regulating the troublesome curves of the nose, the mouth, and the ears. This undoubtedly added to the regularity of the type, but unfortunately not to its beauty. Any attempt at real modelling is scarcely visible, unless it be that the fine lines which are sometimes seen to accompany the sharp, well-marked outline might mean an attempt at shading. In a type of face the linear beauty of which is expressed by the spiral it will not surprise one to find paint, for example, of green or violet applied to heighten the general effect. Regarding the body supposed to belong to this extraordinary head we do not see much of it, as it is usually hidden by a long robe or drapery, ornamented in various ways. Occasionally the whole thing is treated much in the same manner as the compartment of an initial, and filled in with spirals, fret work, or interlacings. Or, this more elaborate ornament is confined to smaller sections only or entirely displaced by some plainer pattern, the mass of the drapery being worked, for example, with a diapered design of lines and dots, while, at the same time, its folds are made visible. This is effected, not by shading, but by streaks of paint of a different colour from that in which the mass of the drapery is painted. The intensely decorative treatment shown in the surface enrichments, in the spiral details, and the impossible colours of the human figure, also characterises the representations of animal forms. Here it is, if possible, even more conspicuous. The spiral recurs in the ears, jaws, and junctions of the limbs with the body The whole space of the body is frequently covered with an intricate pattern of some of the ordinary types, and the colours are distributed without the slightest regard to nature. An example illustrative of the method of procedure deserves to be recorded. It is taken from a copy of the Gospels dating from the twelfth century and now preserved among the Harleian manuscripts in the British Museum.[1] The figure in question represents the lion of St. Mark. The head is of the conventional type, and the tail foliated. The colours employed are red, white, green, and yellow, the former two being used for the head, while half of the body is painted green, and the other half yellow.

From what has been said about the peculiarities of the Celtic miniatures it will be inferred that they are no masterpieces in way of illustration. And yet they are not so utterly destitute of all artistic merit as some people think. When carefully executed, as in the books of the best period, they often combine very well with the purely ornamental work of the broad surrounding borders, to heighten the decorative effect of the page. And there are miniature pages, as, for example, in the *Book of Kells*[2], where the odd formulæ in which the figures appear are in such a singular harmony with the innermost character of the ornament, and the two elements, miniature and ornament, so admirably united into a consistent whole of most original aspect that we are well justified in speaking of a *style*, with reference to similar productions.

[1] *Harl. MS. 1802*, Brit. Mus.
[2] *MS. A. 1. 6.*, Trinity Coll., Dublin.

D

REFIXED to each of the Gospels in the Celtic §VIII
illuminated copies of the Sacred Word is, as
a rule, a representation of the Evangelist.
This picture occupies a separate page, and
is enclosed within a magnificent border. Occasionally it is accompanied by another miniature
page, which bears the figure of his symbol. Or
the Evangelist and his symbol will be seen inserted in the same page; and in books of later
times and inferior workmanship a simple outline
drawing of the emblem would be deemed sufficient
illustration. Other subjects are of less frequency. In the
Book of Kells there are pictures suggested by Scripture history, representing the Virgin and Child, Christ on the pinnacle of the temple, and Christ seized by the Jews. And in
other instances we meet with a painting of the Crucifixion
or of Christ in Glory. In the Celtic illuminated Psalters,
which seem, so far as decoration is concerned, to have
been less generously treated than the Gospel-books, we
also find some miniatures. David playing on the harp,
David and Goliath, and David rending the jaws of the
lion, are the chief subjects represented in the small paintings that occur at the head of each of the three traditional
sections of Psalms. According to a fashion which seems
to be of high antiquity, and which, in the later Middle
Ages, led to the method of introducing among the miniatures of the Psalter a whole series of paintings illustrative
of the Life of Christ, some additional illustration referring
to the New Testament history would be inserted, the most
common being that of the Crucifixion.

It might be supposed that a school characterised by
the intense Celticism of these and similar productions owed
little or nothing to the art of miniature painting as cultivated outside of the Celtic area. Yet this is not the case.
In spite of a curiously unique style and feeling in design,
the decorative paintings with scriptural subjects which occur in the Celtic Psalters and Gospel-books are not to be
regarded as original inventions, but merely as copies which

are ultimately traceable to non-Celtic models. If we compare, for example, the representations of the Evangelists in the Celtic Gospels with those found in Byzantine or Italo-Byzantine illuminated manuscripts of contemporary or still remoter date, we find a remarkable correspondence in invention combined with striking contrasts in execution. On the one side we have a work which, though belonging to a debased period, still bears the impress of classical art; perfectly intelligible as to its meaning; showing some observation of nature, and treated with as much grace and freedom as might be expected from a style of art languishing under the mosaic *régime*. The Evangelist appears as a man of advanced age. His head, of a careworn but noble type, is surrounded by a golden nimbus, and his body draped in an ecclesiastical robe. He is usually represented seated, writing his Gospel; a desk of a peculiar type, with writing-utensils, is placed at his side, while a drapery and architectural work serve to indicate the nature of the locality. The whole is laid on a golden ground and framed either by a round arch supported by columns or by a highly-ornamental border. Of the four pictures that of St. John is occasionally seen to differ more markedly from the others, inasmuch as it represents a young man seated in a desolate place, writing, while an aged man is seen at his side, lost in contemplation of the celestial secrets which are revealed to him by the »*Dextera Dei*». This is the work of the Byzantine artist. And now turning to the other side, we meet with a fanciful device, which from a comparison with its semi-classical pendant only looks more barbarous than ever, full of defects in design and utterly absurd in colouring, testifying to an absolute incapacity of rendering natural forms naturally. And yet, on a closer inspection, this work will be seen to have so much in common with the other one: in the motive selected, in the pose of the figure, in the shape and arrangement of the drapery, and even in the details of accessories, such as seat, cushion, draped background, etc., that we can scarcely entertain any doubt that they are

126

actually related as model and copy. How this was brought
about has yet to be shown. In dealing with a dim and
distant period of the Middle Ages, we realise the difficulty
of tracing, with anything approaching to accuracy, the
historical lines of intercourse between nations and peoples;
the more so, when we bear in mind that an ample portion of the written records of the day are of the legendary
mould, and, accordingly, should be employed with great
reserve. In a following article, in which the broader
question of the origination of Celtic design in general has
to be treated, it is proposed to pursue further our
research on the descent of the Celtic miniatures,
by adding to the internal evidence such information as can be gathered from authenticated history.

EFORE entering on a discussion of the effect and §IX
value of the peculiar style of art exhibited in
the illuminated manuscripts of the Celtic school,
it was necessary first to pass over the whole
field and try to get a general outlook, by analys-
ing the whole complex growth of Celtic ornament and classifying its different elements. This
done, we are in a position more keenly to discern
the characteristics of the separate groups and also to
grasp better the effect of the *ensemble*. And we are bound
to say, the peculiar beauty of this style of ornament
chiefly depends on the *ensemble*. Although showing a
variety of forms, which testify to the admirable capacity
of the designer both in invention and execution, yet the
separate element of decoration gains its real significance,
only when grouped together with other motives in a composite scheme. The Celtic illuminator was well aware of
that, and, accordingly, tried to the best of his powers to
combine his patterns so as to produce a rich and pleasing
effect. And it must be admitted that his faculty of artistic
composition was assuredly not inferior either to his fer-
tility of invention or to his executive skill.

His method was to divide the surface to be decorated,
whether it was the whole space of a page, or the long,

narrow band of a border, or the irregularly shaped body of an initial, into a series of sections and afterwards to fill in each of these with a pattern of its own. The shape of the divisions, separated from each other by means of marginal lines, was partly ruled by the outline of the space to be divided. Thus, while the all-round border and the full-page decoration, delineated on a strictly rectangular plan, usually present a series of panels of square, oblong, or otherwise rectangular shape, compartments bounded by curved lines, alternating with rectilinear panels, were dictated by the outline of the large irregular initial or of the partial border. The manner in which the pattern is selected and adjusted to suit the shape of the panel or compartment reveals a considerable amount of skill and taste. Spirals were chiefly used to fill in the irregular sections of the body of the letter and its curvilinear en-closed spaces, where, owing to a certain freedom in fixing the centres and making volutes of varying size, they were easily adapted and in keeping with the flowing outline of the margin. Interlacements were less easily adapted, but could be made to suit an irregular space, for instance, by forming a chain of knots of varying size and intricacy; whereas fret patterns were even more rarely used outside of the square or oblong panels, for which they were natu-rally suited. Thus the disposal of the various designs was ruled by taste, and actually effected what it aimed at, viz., the combination of contrasting elements in a graceful scheme. In pages where the ornament groups round a well-defined centre there is a tendency towards symmetrical arrangement. This is shown, for example, in miniature-pages that have a broad ornamental border run right round the picture of the Evangelist or that of his symbol. But the most beautiful example of symmetrical composition, uniting a pleasing variety of details with solid structure, is supplied by the page, entirely overgrown with orna-ment supported by a cruciform design, which is generally seen to precede the initial page.

In a Gospel-book of the richest type we have no

fewer than four highly-decorative pages placed at the commencement of each Gospel. First, there is a page containing the picture of the Evangelist, enclosed within an elaborate border; next, there is one containing his symbol, also with border work; then, there is a full ornamental page with the cruciform design to which we have just referred; and, lastly, we have the initial page, in which the first words of the Gospel are painted or written in characters of more or less decorative aspect. First among these in size and splendour is the initial, often extending to the full height of the page. Occasionally an all-round border, similar to those of the preceding leaves, may be seen also in this page. But often the ornamented body of the initial was deemed sufficient decoration for the one half of the page, and a particular border only designed for the other half so as to meet the extremities of the initial and supplement it with corner-pieces in the vacancies. In the space left between border and initial there are rows of letters which gradually decrease in height and decoration until they pass into ordinary characters. In addition to these there are one or two other pages which received special attention, the principal being that — in the Gospel of St. Matthew — in which the verse: » *XPI autem generatio sic erat*», offered its monogrammatic contraction of the name of Christ to decorative treatment. The page is arranged much in the same manner as the ordinary initial page. The monogram is drawn in letters of bold, magnificent outline, and brilliantly ornamented. There is a beautiful instance in the *Book of Kells*, presumably surpassing, as a piece of decoration, anything to be met with in any other written book. It is a page to discourage even the most accomplished and most enthusiastic of modern draughtsmen. In nine cases out of ten he will break down before his work is half finished; or, if he should really succeed in completing it, he will have to expend upon it an amount of time and labour out of all proportion to the apparent result of his work. Mr. Digby Wyatt made an attempt, and had to give it up. Professor J. O. Westwood, who was a great admirer of Irish art and at the same time a skilled draughtsman, went to work with no better result. And he was assuredly not one to be discouraged by difficulties arising from variety of colours and intricacy of design. No one who has had an opportunity of examining the leaves of the big volume containing the Professor's original tracings and now deposited in the Ashmolean Museum at Oxford, can have failed to be struck by the minute accuracy of his delineations and the immense pains taken in rendering even the most complicated passages of Celtic ornament. And yet the copying of the monogram page of the *Book of Kells* was, if not beyond his powers, at least too long and serious an affair to be duly brought to completion. We are indebted to Miss Margaret Stokes, the accomplished writer on Celtic antiquities, for possessing, at last, a copy[1] perfectly finished and worthy of an original which the same author, in a brilliant passage referring to its unique variety of design, has signalised as »an epitome of Irish art».[2]

Before leaving the ornamental compositions in the illuminated copies of the Gospels, we must not omit mention of the frame work enclosing the Eusebian Canons. Occasionally it appears in the traditional form of a series of arches supported by columns and spanned by a superior arch. Or the whole is confined to a border carried all round the page. In both cases the patterns employed are of the ordinary types; and the Celtic fashion of treating any space to be decorated as a flat surface, reappears in the decoration of the columns, with shafts, bases, and capitals enriched on the panel principle.

Of illuminated Psalters now extant there are none to equal the finest Gospel-books, so far as decoration is concerned. They are smaller in size, less carefully executed, and, in their ornament and character of writing, present

[1] Now deposited in the National Museum of Ireland, Dublin; a chromo-lithographic reproduction, which, however, as to softness and harmony of colour leaves much to be desired, may be seen in *Vetusta Monumenta*, vol. VI, plate I.
[2] Margaret Stokes, *Early Christian art in Ireland*, London, 1887, p. 13.

features that enable us to assign them, with one or two exceptions, to a period when the art of book-illumination had passed its culminating point. An ornamental initial will be seen at the head of each of the three divisions of Psalms; and a leaf with a picture is occasionally prefixed to each section.

§ X

OLOUR as a means of heightening decorative effect was made a liberal use of in Irish art. At an early period the native of the Isle knew how to relieve the sombre tone of his bronzes by the use of *champ- levé* enamel. And in the Christian era he possessed a variety of methods of work by which he was able to impart a picturesque appearance even to a material which does not readily admit of much variation in that point. There are still extant, in fairly good preservation and sufficient numbers, specimens of Irish metal work of the Christian centuries, showing how much he revelled in bright and varied colours in that class of work; and how manifold and ingenious were his devices in effecting pleasing contrasts of colour. One was to combine in the manufacture of the work different metals or alloys. Thus in many cases we find three, four, or even five different metals applied for constructive and decorative purposes, gold and silver being added to bronze and simpler materials. This method, dictated by judicious economy, contributed in no small degree to the introduction of a pleasing picturesque variety. Small golden panels ornamented with twisted or granulated rods and minute patterns of most exquisite workmanship were fixed on, for example, to a surface of silver, with a finer effect than could ever be produced by the same kind of work if entirely wrought in gold. Or a plate of metal with a pierced pattern was rivetted on another plate in such a manner that the surface of the latter became partly visible through the openings. Then, there were the various methods of enamelling, of gilding, and bronzing, of inlaying with niello; the settings of coloured glasses, crystals, and pieces of amber; all tending to enliven and beautify by contrast of colour.

In this connexion, though only concerned with the Celtic metal work in its polychromatic aspect, we can not refrain from a remark in passing. And that is that the crude notion of the value of an *objet d'art* — especially in the case of metal work — as being chiefly dependent on the richness and splendour of the material employed, will never be more readily abandoned than in studying the productions of the Celtic school of metal workers. What lends to their work its value is certainly not the weight of precious metal spent on it, or any matchless brilliancy of the materials used for the settings. Compared with an Eastern work, heavy with gold and set with rubies and amethysts, the Celtic work would look very poor, indeed, so far as material is concerned; composed as it is, in its main mass, of some plainer metal, with coloured glasses, pieces of amber, and rock-crystals — rather than rubies and amethysts. And yet, from the point of view of art, how immensely superior is a work in which, like the Celtic specimen, a poorer stuff is ennobled by judicious arrangement in structure and refinement of taste in decoration to that which chiefly owes its significance to the costliness of the material, as do so many gorgeous products of Oriental art.

Mr. Henry O'Neill, in his work on the *high crosses* of Ireland, has expressed an opinion that the patterns cut in relief on these beautiful specimens of ancient Irish stone sculpture were intended to receive a finishing touch by polychromatic treatment.[1] When we consider what a great part colour plays in Irish ornament, we must admit his assumption to have at least some show of reason; but, on the other hand, as there is no trace of colour left to support his theory, it may be well to leave the question an open one.

[1] *Illustrations of the most interesting of the sculptured crosses of Ancient Ireland;* drawn to scale and lithographed by Henry O'Neill; London, 1857; Introduction, p. III; *cfr. The fine arts and civilization of Ancient Ireland,* by the same author; London, 1863, p. 72.

E

In no class of works, however, produced by Celtic artificers has the love of colour found a more perfect and more beautiful expression than in the pages of the illuminated manuscripts. It is not easy to decide what is most to be admired in these, the delicate touch and facile dexterity in designing, or the exquisite colouring. Among the colours applied to the decoration of the finer specimens there are black and white in addition to the whole series of the spectrum, from a fiery red to the deepest ultramarine and violet. Moreover, there are shades of the same colour differing in tone and depth. More particularly is such the case with the green, the yellow, and the violet, which colours are varied and combined with special grace and treated throughout *con amore*. A very full set of colours will, not infrequently, be seen exhibited in the same page. Gold is very rare. It occurs in the *Gospels of Lindisfarne*, where it is used very sparingly for some small circular dots and triangular interstices; but in manuscripts written in the native Isle it is practically unknown. It is doubtful whether the Irish illuminators knew the practice of silver and bronze applications. Occasionally a reddish or brownish colour so closely agrees with the tone of the latter material that it might, at first sight, be mistaken for a metal application.

The general effect produced by an illuminated page is largely dependent on the prevalence of the darker or brighter elements. Thus there is a very marked difference in tone and feeling between, for example, a decorated page in the *Gospels of Lindisfarne*, with its light, gay colours, and a corresponding page in the *Book of Kells*, in which the darker and heavier tones are predominant. Hence, a sparkling brightness on the one side; on the other a certain sombre dignity. In examining more closely an illuminated page we notice one point of special significance. And that is the masterly way in which the colours are selected and distributed with a view to make the most of the design, and at the same time combined so as to keep in perfect harmony with each other. Considering the minute and delicate nature of the design, one might think, the introduction of colour would make the pattern disappear, and the whole result in a confused mass of pigments. But this is far from being the case. On the contrary, the colours are applied in such a way as to make even the most minute pattern come out beautifully clear and distinct. One method was to introduce a strong contrast between pattern and background. By a black or dark ground, which is very common, and may be said to be a rule in the best works, a pattern painted in brighter colours, even if it be of minute proportions, will be seen to be raised in a most effective manner. A further means of emphasising the outline of the design was to run a fine edging of a very light tint, usually white or yellow, along the contour; and thus cut it, so to say, out of its ground. This method of edging an outline with a fine band of a strongly contrasting colour is a characteristic feature of Celtic illumination, and, simple though it is, contributes in no small degree to the pleasing distinctness of its details. In being applied to the marginal lines which enclose the separate panel, as well as to the still broader margins of the whole body of an initial or a border, it affects the composition of the whole complex ornament, by rendering the outline of the chief divisions, as well as of the whole mass, strong and clear. Another characteristic may be seen in the row of dots accompanying the outline of the initial. Occasionally it extends to embrace whole rows of letters in the same page. In this case the vacant spaces intervening between the letters, and also the enclosed parts of the letters used to be filled in altogether with rows of dots, more or less regularly disposed; or with the scheme of a fret, interlaced, or zoomorphic motive, punctured out on the same principle. The dotted lines and patterns are mostly in red.

Geometrical interlacings were often painted in sections of alternating colours, like chequer work; and the same method is occasionally seen to have been followed also in the case of fret work. But in no group of patterns was colour applied with a finer effect than in the case of spirals. The small sections worked with these designs afford, in fact, the most exquisite details of decoration to be met with in Celtic art. A pattern of quadruple spirals designed on the minute scale of Celtic book-decoration is rather a mysterious affair, hardly intelligible as an ornament. But thanks to a judicious application of a variety of vivid colours and the unfailing precision with which pattern and background are made to contrast, the ornament comes out as distinctly as might be desired. In this way the whole of the space to be illuminated, even in its smallest interstices, is gradually laid with pigments; and an ornamental composition of unrivalled merit, equally finished in design and colouring, is the final result of long painstaking and devoted labours.

The pigments, carefully prepared according to formulæ the secrets of which are unfortunately lost to modern manufacture, still retain, in many cases, a great deal of their original force and lustre. Even in pages so worn and blackened by age and vicissitudes as to be all but illegible, the tints of the colouring can still be made out from patches left. And there are those, unaffected by age and accidents, in which everything, vellum, writing, and colouring, is so beautifully clean and fresh that you might hold it a work of yesterday, were it not for the strange-looking type of letter and the quaint and queer old ornament. Such a book is the manuscript known as the *Gospels of Lindisfarne* or the *Book of Durham*, which was written twelve centuries ago. There is one other point worthy of notice, before we leave the subject of colour. And that is the very liberal way in which the paint was laid on. There are pages in which the pigments are, in fact, so lavishly applied as almost to raise the pattern in relief. The effect produced by such a work, with its lustrous, thickly-laid pigments, occasionally recalls that of a minute Venetian mosaic or some highly-finished enamel work. Some fine examples may be seen in a dainty little copy of the Gospels, now one of the chief treasures of the Archiepiscopal library at Lambeth[1]; and some others of still higher perfection meet us in the pages of the often-mentioned famous production of the School of Lindisfarne[2]. A good photograph will render even the most minute details of the ornament, so far ·as its linear element goes, with all desirable accuracy; but there is no mechanical process among those hitherto invented that can give an adequate idea of such an illumination in its picturesque aspect. A chromo-lithographic reproduction, even if carefully prepared, seldom catches the tone and feeling of the original, or gives us more than an approximate resemblance. This is true more especially with reference to the attempts that have been made to reproduce in print the colours of Celtic illuminations. We have to turn to the manuscript itself if we want to judge fairly of its merits and realise the lustre, softness, and harmony of its ornament.

MONG the ancient documents preserved in the library of Trinity College in Dublin is an illuminated volume of large quarto size containing the Four Gospels, mainly in accordance with the Vulgate version , and generally known as the *Book of Kells*[5] (see *National MSS. Irel.*, vol. I, plates VII—XVII; Westwood, *Miniatures and Ornaments,* plates VIII—XI; *Palæographia,* plates 16, 17; *Celtic Ornaments from the Book of Kells,* vols. I—IX). On account of the lavish abundance and exceptional perfection of its artistic work this book is justly regarded, not only as the chief treasure in this precious collection, but also as by far the costliest relic of ancient Celtic art that has come down to our time. It is known to have formerly belonged to the monastery of Cenannus, or Kells, in Meath; hence, its name. At the commencement and the end of the volume some smaller portions are missing; but leaving this defect out of account, we may say that the manuscript has descended to us in a very good state of preservation. In pages which were originally left blank, records referring to the ecclesiastical community of Kells have been entered at an early period; but there is no colophon nor signature left to tell us the name of the scribe or the circumstances under which the work was produced. If there ever was anything of the kind, it may have disappeared together with the fragments missing at the end of the manuscript. The text is written throughout in a remarkably clear and regular hand; a few pages (26 recto and verso, 29 verso—31 recto) being in double columns. At the commencement some pages are written in lines of black and red alternating, while the rest of the text is in a black or brownish ink.

As to the artistic enrichment of the volume, this manuscript equals the Lindisfarne Gospels in accuracy of drawing, and softness and harmony of colour, and surpasses it in the lavish abundance and astounding variety of its ornament. Almost every page may be said to show decorative features. At the commencement of each of the Gospels we meet with a series of grand illuminated pages, including the picture of the Evangelist, a full-page composition of the four symbols, an ornamental page with a

cruciform design, and the page containing the first words of the Gospel; all of which are worked with a variety of design and colouring, and a perfection and finish of detail, of which no literal description can give an adequate idea. Then, there are the decorative framings of the Eusebian Canons; the marvellously ornamented page marking the passage: ›*XPI autem generatio sic erat*‹, St. Matthew I, 18; and — a thing of rare occurrence in the Celtic copies of the Gospels — a series of full-page miniatures, with subjects suggested by the accompanying text. Thus we see the *Virgin and Child,* surrounded by angels; the *Temptation:* Jesus on the pinnacle of the temple; and *Jesus seized by the Jews;* the first two of which are enclosed within elaborate square borders, while the last-mentioned scene is set between two columns spanned by a round arch. In addition to these pages, illuminations of hardly less elaborate character are seen to be inserted in the sequence of chapters, to mark some passage or other which seemed to be of special importance; and minor decorations, in an amazing variety of forms, appear in every page throughout the volume, being used as terminals, or as fancy-flourishes appended to plain letters, or as initials placed at the head of every new sentence.

It is evident that the ornamental work, at least to some extent, was executed after the text was completed. Some of the smaller initials are left unfinished; and in the border work framing the double columns, fol. 29 verso—31 recto, only small portions are executed in colours and patterns, while the rest is drawn in outline only. Among the patterns employed there are first the whole series of those typical of Celtic art and of frequent occurrence in the earlier manuscripts, such as geometrical fret, interlaced, and spiral patterns, together with zoomorphic interlacements in every possible variety of form and composition. But besides these we notice an admixture of elements some of which are rarely, if ever, met with in Celtic art outside of these pages. Among these novelties we find, for example, several varieties of chequer and tesselated pattern, generally introduced to enliven smaller spaces and vacancies intervening between the broader and more elaborate designs. Then, there are various forms of the rosette, a type of ornament which is decidedly un-Celtic. Among the minor decorations inserted throughout the ordinary text, at the beginning or the end of the line, or in the vacant spaces left between two sentences, we have figures of birds, quadrupeds, fishes, serpents, warrior armed with shield and spear, man on horseback, etc., together with fancy-flourishes in almost unlimited variety; the whole

1 Henry O'Neill, *The Sculptured Crosses of Ancient Ireland,* plate 29.
2 *Op. cit.,* plate 25.
3 *Op. cit.,* plates 10, 14, 15.
4 *Histoire de la Vulgate,* pp. 41, 42.
5 *MS. A. I. 6.,* Trinity Coll., Dublin.

betraying an effort after enrichment which to modern eyes is somewhat childish and bizarre in its general effect. But the most important innovation is the introduction of foliage. This element appears, to begin with, among the flourishes and terminals, in the shape of lightly sketched branches with leaves and flowers, sometimes proceeding from vases. Of a more elaborate nature are the scrolls of foliage which are seen to fill in, as a surface decoration, long, narrow borders or panels in the grand illuminated pages. The most characteristic form is a pattern of a single wavy stem with alternate recurved scrolls terminating in trefoil-shaped leaves. Also in this position the stem is occasionally found to proceed from a vase. More general, however, is a less rational connexion of leaf design with zoomorphic patterns. Thus a branch of foliage is frequently seen to evolve from between the open jaws of a nondescript, while at the same time the tail of the beast presents the appearance of a trefoil or lancet-shaped leaf. And there are other patterns in which zoomorphic forms are intertwined with undulating stems of foliage, much on the same principle as the compositions which, in the previous pages, we have observed in dialects of non-Celtic decorative art. As an example of the freedom and variety displayed in the illumination of the manuscript we may note two pages facing each other, fol. 145 verso—146 recto. In these the illuminated initial combination *Et* occurs no less than seven times, in forms all of which vary in outline and colouring. Moreover, the same combination appears repeatedly throughout the text, but there is no one instance of it that can be said to be a mechanical repetition of a foregoing form.

Concerning the age of the manuscript nothing is known with certainty. The current theory, based on an ancient tradition, has, however, assigned it to a very remote period. In the *Annals of Ulster* a record under the year 1006 refers to a remarkable manuscript which at that time belonged to the church of Kells. It reads as follows:

»— — The great Gospel of Colum-Cille was wickedly stolen in the night out of the western sacristy of the great stone-church of Cenannas — the chief relic of the western world, on account of its ornamental cover. The same Gospel was found after twenty [nights] and two months, its gold having been taken off it, and a sod over it. — —»[1]

Now the present volume is held to be the very book which, at the commencement of the eleventh century, belonged to the religious establishment at Kells, and was at that time connected by local tradition with the name of St. Columba. And modern authorities like Professor J. O. Westwood[2] and Dr J. H. Todd[3] seem inclined to accept the tradition as historical; and, accordingly, arrive at the conclusion that the still extant manuscript may be regarded as a relic of the days of the Saint of Iona. On the other hand, Dr Joseph Anderson, in his lectures on early Christian Scottish antiquities, refers to the appearance of foliageous ornament in this manuscript as »one indication of its being the product, not of the beginning, but of the culmination of the school of art which it represents».[4] And Miss Margaret Stokes, who has perhaps devoted to this volume more study than anyone else, in her later publications, expresses an opinion that it was executed as late as the ninth century.[5] We think there is something to be said for the last-mentioned hypothesis. And we hope to show in a following article, in which the characteristics of the Carlovingian art are to be considered, that there exist, in fact, between the non-Celtic elements of decoration shown in the *Book of Kells* and the art dialect just alluded to, such affinities as will hardly leave room for doubt that the Celtic manuscript was produced under the influence of that early *renaissance* which commenced in the Frankish Empire under the reign of Charlemagne.

[1] An. U., A. D. 1006.
[2] *Palæographia*, Book of Kells, p. 6; *Miniatures and Ornaments*, p. 26.
[3] *Vetusta Monumenta*, vol. VI, p. 6.
[4] *Scotland in Early Christian times*, vol. I, p. 153.
[5] *Christian Inscriptions*, vol. II, p. 169.